104

TEXT BY
ILLUSTRATIONS BY
DAVID A. ANDERTON | RIKYU WATANABE

HELLCAT

Crown Publishers, Inc.
New York

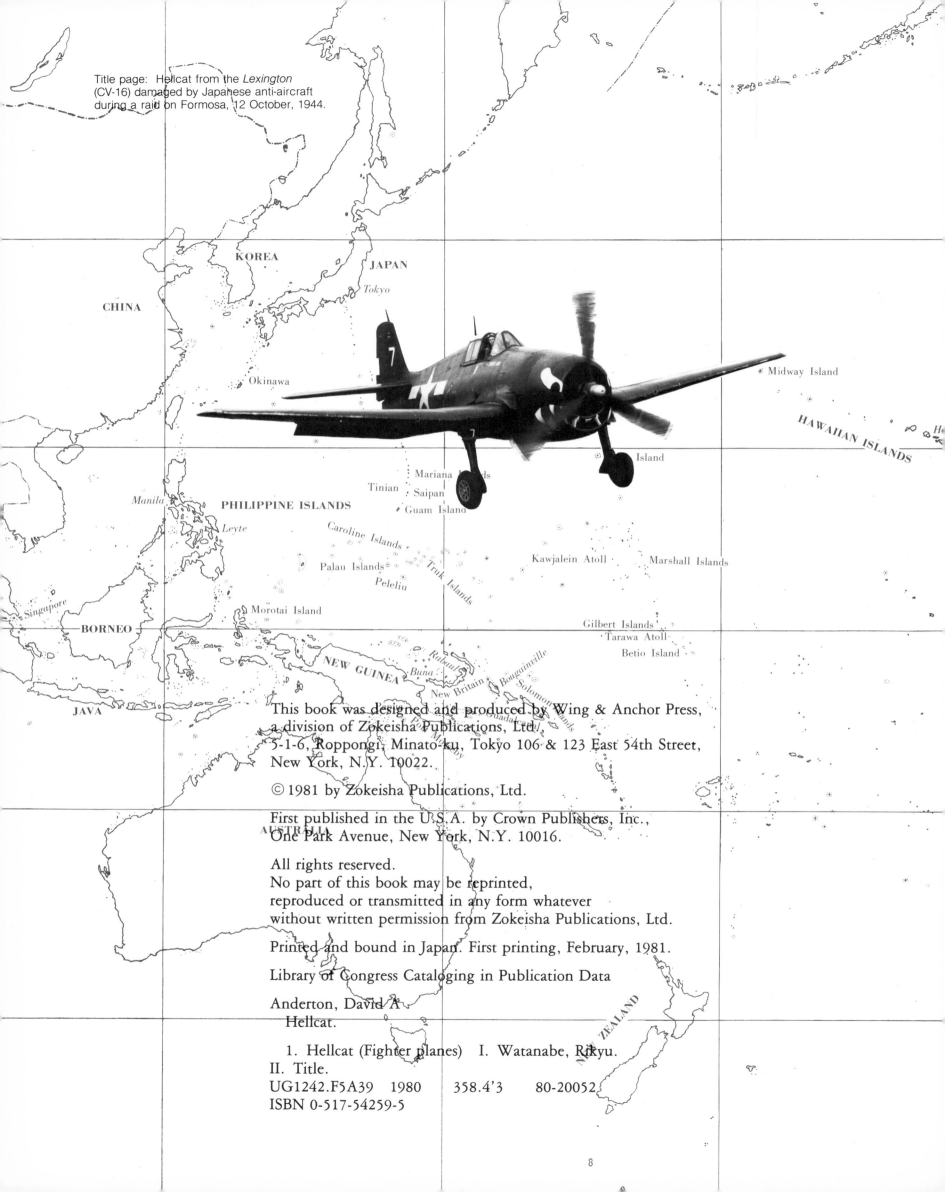

Title page: Hellcat from the *Lexington* (CV-16) damaged by Japanese anti-aircraft during a raid on Formosa, 12 October, 1944.

This book was designed and produced by Wing & Anchor Press, a division of Zokeisha Publications, Ltd. 5-1-6, Roppongi, Minato-ku, Tokyo 106 & 123 East 54th Street, New York, N.Y. 10022.

First published in the U.S.A. by Crown Publishers, Inc., One Park Avenue, New York, N.Y. 10016.

Printed and bound in Japan. First printing, February, 1981.

Library of Congress Cataloging in Publication Data

Anderton, David A
Hellcat.

1. Hellcat (Fighter planes) I. Watanabe, Rikyu.
II. Title.
UG1242.F5A39   1980   358.4'3   80-20052
ISBN 0-517-54259-5

"A Bigger and Better Wildcat..."

An F6F-3N, factory-fresh, on the aft deck of the *Charger*. October, 1943.

A dozen humpbacked Hellcats cruised the high skies above the Pacific atoll of Tarawa on 23 November, 1943. With engines cut back to their most efficient cruise power settings, the twelve Grummans orbited in a steady racetrack flight pattern. The midday sun flooded into the cockpits through the canopies, lighting the side consoles. Crazy-house mirror images of portions of flight suits, arms and hands danced on the inner surfaces of the canopy and windshield, and rebounded from the small faces of the instruments.

"Fighting Sixteen", skippered by Lt. Cdr. Paul D. Buie, was flying combat air patrol, a defensive screen for its carrier, the USS *Lexington*, and other ships in the task force lying in the waters off the atoll.

The taking of Tarawa had been assigned to an amphibious assault force of U.S. Marines. They stormed the beach, established a beachhead, and doggedly moved inland, taking fierce fire from the Japanese defenders. Cornered on the atoll, the trapped Japanese made a last desperate charge during the night of 22 November. Now it was about noon on the following day, and the Marines were still moving methodically through the ruined defences, flushing out individual Japanese soldiers. It would take another day to complete their task, but by then the ground defences on the atoll had crumbled.

There was still Japanese air strength to reckon with, long-range bombers and torpedo aircraft, escorted by the agile Zero, dog-fighter supreme in the Pacific skies, and a most effective fighter-bomber besides. That threat, if it appeared, was the reason for the flight of Hellcats assigned to combat air patrol (CAP).

Picket destroyers cruised well offshore, far below the fighters; their radars searched the alloted sectors of sky out to the limits of their sightlines, watching for the telltale echoes that would signal the impending arrival of a Japanese air strike.

"Bogies!", said one of the radar operators, spotting the first signs of a return on the circular screen that played back the patterns seen by the rotating antennae. Other obser-

vers confirmed the sighting, and concentrated their attention on the motion and direction of the luminous blob on the screen.

It advanced, and began to break into a clearly discernible formation of aircraft. There were no incoming signals from IFF (Identification, Friend or Foe) systems that now were standard in the U.S. fleet. They were Japanese, 21 of them, probably fighter-bombers escorted by fighters. And that meant a sky full of Zeros.

The Fighter Director Officer on board the destroyer vectored Buie's squadron toward the incoming strike. They were at altitude, and up-sun from the Japanese, in a classical offensive position of advantage for the attacker. The Hellcats, flying at about 23,000 feet (7000 m) were at least 4,000 feet (1220 m) above the incoming force.

The distance between the two air units closed; Buie called the tallyho, rolled and ruddered his Hellcat toward the "Zekes" and "Hamps," followed by eleven eager Navy pilots looking for a good fight.

They got it. They tore into the Japanese formation in a high-sided, overhead attack that flamed a few of the Zeros on the first pass. And then the sky was filled with individual combats, flashes of white stars and red suns, dark blue fuselages and wings chasing blue-green shapes with polished black cowlings, spurts of flame from wing leading edges and atop cowlings, longer tongues of flame blossoming into great gouts of fire and smoke. Here and there a parachute, pilot dangling below, headed for the water.

The fight raged for ten minutes, between 23,000 feet (7000 m) and about a mile above the Pacific's rolling swells. When it was over, only the Hellcats remained in the air, in complete control of the skies over Tarawa. No Navy pilots had been lost in the swirling combat; they had learned how to fight with their Hellcats, and particularly how not to fight with the nimble Zeros. Don't ever dogfight with those guys, they had been told, or you will be dead. Use your power, your speed, and your altitude advantage to get them on the first pass; if they get on your tail, roll and dive fast, You'll make it OK.

Lt. (jg) Ralph Hanks had learned well. It was his first real combat, and he was now an ace. He got five Zeros in about five minutes, the first of many Navy pilots who were to make ace in a single engagement.

24 November saw action again in the same arena with the same combatants. But on that day, the Japanese entered the scene with an altitude advantage. They did not exploit it properly and, within minutes, they were caught in a replay of the previous day's slaughter. The Hellcats shot down 13 of the attacking force, and claimed credit for six more. One Hellcat pilot was killed in the combat.

The two engagements added up to a remarkable record for the Hellcat. From the beginning it had been designed to kill Zeros, and it was doing just that. In these two fights, U.S. Navy pilots had downed 30 Zeros certainly, ten more probably, and had lost one of their own. The kill ratio was an impressive 30 to one. It was the pattern, if not the dimension, of the Hellcat's combat record during its action in the Pacific.

Genesis of the Hellcat

The design process that produced the Grumman F6F series of Hellcat fighters was evolutionary, rather than revolutionary. It had its roots in the early wartime combat experience of its immediate predecessor in U.S. Navy service, the Grumman F4F-3 Wildcat. Those tubby fighters were front-line equipment on Navy carriers and with Marine land-based units when war broke out on 7 December, 1941. They had the expected modest performance of a fighter that had been

recognized by an anonymous cartoonist at Grumman who, soon after the Hellcat was a matter of public knowledge, drew an arrogant-looking Hellcat being told by a self-righteous Wildcat, "Hellcat, Hell! Copycat!"

The resemblance was not accidental, either at Grumman or at the home of any other aircraft line that is developed. But it was part of the basic Grumman design philosophy, which required the designers to "Make it strong, make it work, and make it simple." Known components give more confidence in their operation than do unknown ones, so Grumman – and other companies – built successive generations of fighters on the lines of the predecessors.

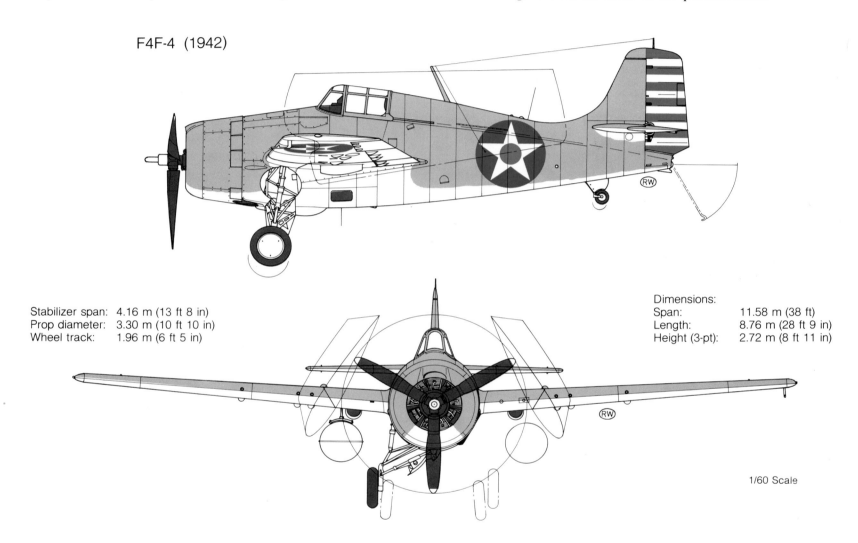

F4F-4 (1942)

Stabilizer span: 4.16 m (13 ft 8 in)
Prop diameter: 3.30 m (10 ft 10 in)
Wheel track: 1.96 m (6 ft 5 in)

Dimensions:
Span: 11.58 m (38 ft)
Length: 8.76 m (28 ft 9 in)
Height (3-pt): 2.72 m (8 ft 11 in)

1/60 Scale

designed in the mid-1930s, and the first and most obvious way to improve that performance was to fit an engine of increased horsepower.

Faded Grumman blueprints and ozalid copies of original design drawings show the gradual evolution of the Hellcat. The requirement for more horsepower led to the use of a larger propeller to absorb the greater horsepower. Increased propeller diameter meant that the landing gear had to be taller, to give sufficient ground clearance. A heavier powerplant demanded more wing area, and a physically larger wing was reflected in the increased areas of vertical and horizontal tail surfaces.

Thus Grumman's proposal to the Navy was an entirely new fighter, no longer a modified Wildcat, but still bearing a definite family resemblance. That similarity was

There were a couple of other guiding principles that every new designer at Grumman soon learned. The first was Roy Grumman's idea: The last part of a Grumman aircraft to fail was to be the cockpit. Grumman, himself a qualified pilot with years of experience, wanted to give Navy pilots the best possible chance to survive the accidentally destructive landing or minor crash. The second was called the "Schwendler factor", after Grumman's chief engineer, William T. Schwendler. It was based on the quite simple principle that if something was strong enough according to the specifications, it surely wouldn't hurt to make it twice as strong. In that case, the designer applied a "Schwendler factor" of 2, and the resulting piece easily met Navy specifications.

Schwendler also told the story of the Hellcat's evolution in an article in the Grumman plant newspaper,

Plane News, for 16 September, 1943. In the first official announcement of the Hellcat, he wrote:

"The Grumman Hellcat – which Grumman men and women have been turning out in such large numbers – bears the distinction of being the first U.S. fighter plane designed and produced in quantity since Pearl Harbor.

"The early Pacific battles – Coral Sea, Marshall and Gilbert Islands, defense of Midway and the attack and conquest of Guadalcanal – all served to write, through experience, the requirements for the type of fighter most needed by the Navy. The Hellcat's specifications were roughly drafted in those distant parts of the Pacific by such men as Thach,

describe what was, simply, the best carrier-based fighter ever developed and built.

It had been designed and built specifically for one kind of war – fighter versus fighter. And fighter meant even more specifically, the Japanese Mitsubishi Zero. It was developed with the thought that it would be flown by a large number of relatively inexperienced, young pilots who needed a forgiving aircraft in the demanding environment of Naval air warfare. And, thought the Grumman officials, if it is going to be built, we're going to need an awful lot of them, so let's make it easy to produce.

The Hellcat was a forgiving aircraft, easy to fight with. It was an excellent gunnery platform, stable and con-

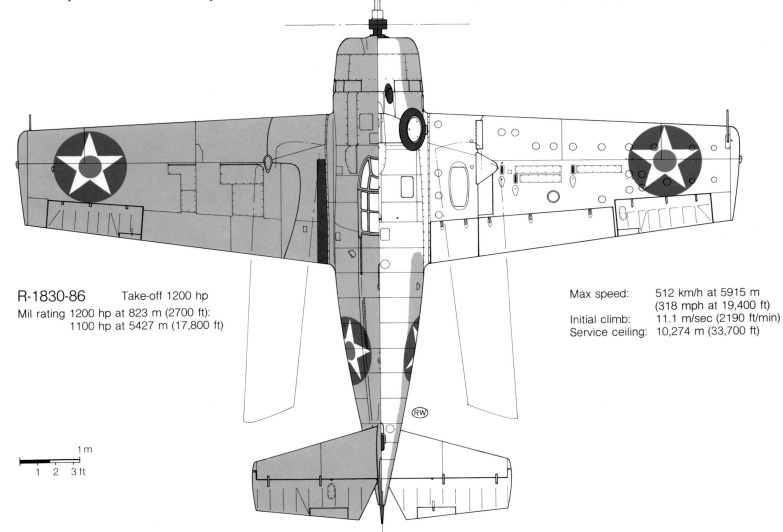

R-1830-86   Take-off 1200 hp
Mil rating 1200 hp at 823 m (2700 ft):
          1100 hp at 5427 m (17,800 ft)

Max speed: 512 km/h at 5915 m
                  (318 mph at 19,400 ft)
Initial climb: 11.1 m/sec (2190 ft/min)
Service ceiling: 10,274 m (33,700 ft)

1 m
1 2 3 ft

Flatley, O'Hare and Gaylor of the Navy and Smith and Carl of the Marines.

"With the insistent demands of these men as the basic design objective, the Hellcat airplane was engineered to provide greater rate of climb and increased speed over that of the Wildcat, heavier fire power and more and better disposed armor protection for both the pilot and vital parts of the airplane." There was a little licence in that statement. The Grumman reports and specification for the XF6F-1 were dated 24 February, 1941; those for the F6F-3 1 August, 1941. Both dates were well before Pearl Harbor, so that very little input of the Pacific combat could have been an initial design influence. But the details of long-forgotten contracts and specifications are unimportant. What remains is the record of the Hellcat, and the words and phrases that only begin to

trollable. It was rugged; its great strength and its ability to take punishment were legends in the fleet. It was easy to maintain, consistently setting the highest availability marks in the fleet. A very high percentage of Hellcats – between 90 and 95 per cent – was always ready for operations. No other Naval aircraft of its time could make that claim, and probably none since.

It ended the war with a kill ratio of 19:1, another mark that has not since been touched. Nor was it within reach of any other fighter at the time.

It was, in every respect, an absolutely remarkable aircraft, and one that can safely be called unmatched.

This is the story of the Grumman F6F Hellcat series, and how they won the Naval air war in the Pacific in World War II.

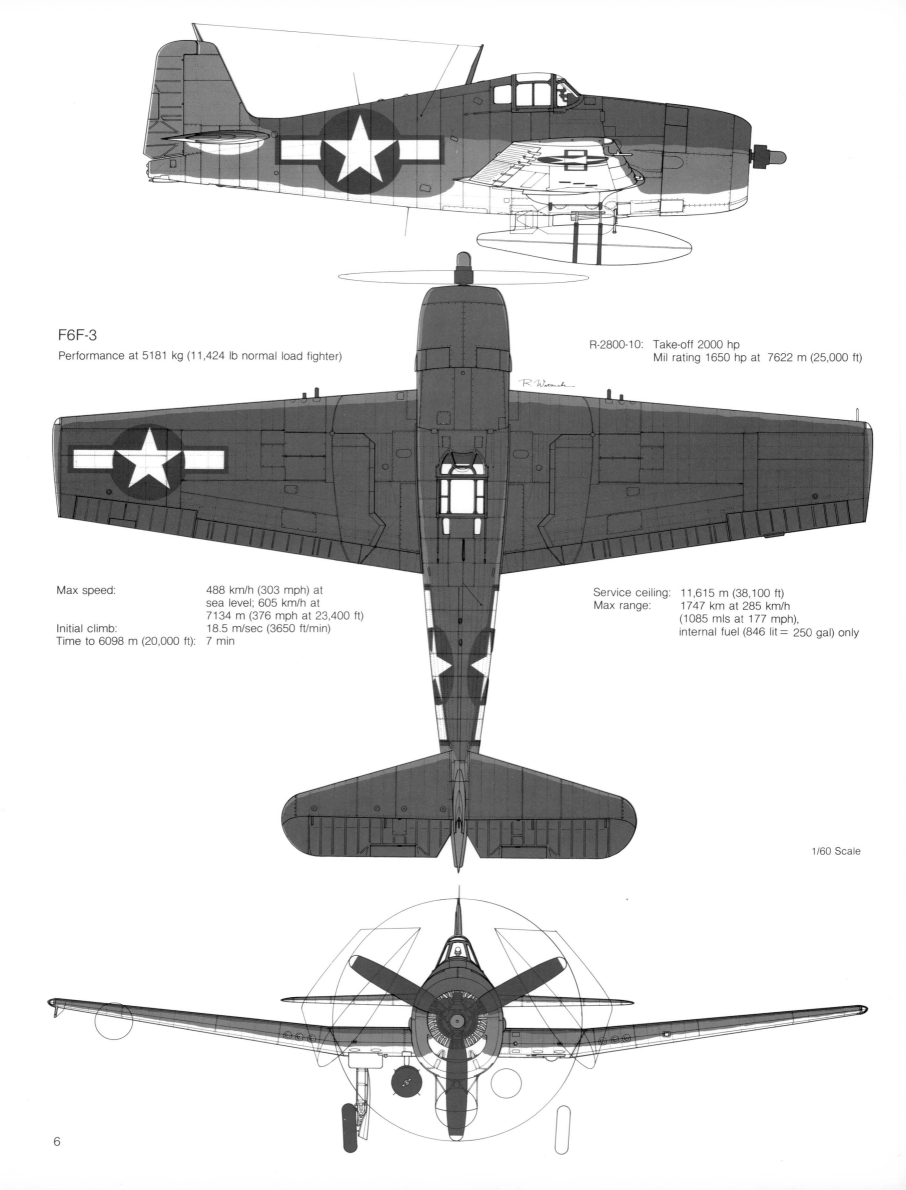

F6F-3

Performance at 5181 kg (11,424 lb normal load fighter)

R-2800-10: Take-off 2000 hp
Mil rating 1650 hp at 7622 m (25,000 ft)

Max speed: 488 km/h (303 mph) at
sea level; 605 km/h at
7134 m (376 mph at 23,400 ft)
Initial climb: 18.5 m/sec (3650 ft/min)
Time to 6098 m (20,000 ft): 7 min

Service ceiling: 11,615 m (38,100 ft)
Max range: 1747 km at 285 km/h
(1085 mls at 177 mph),
internal fuel (846 lit = 250 gal) only

1/60 Scale

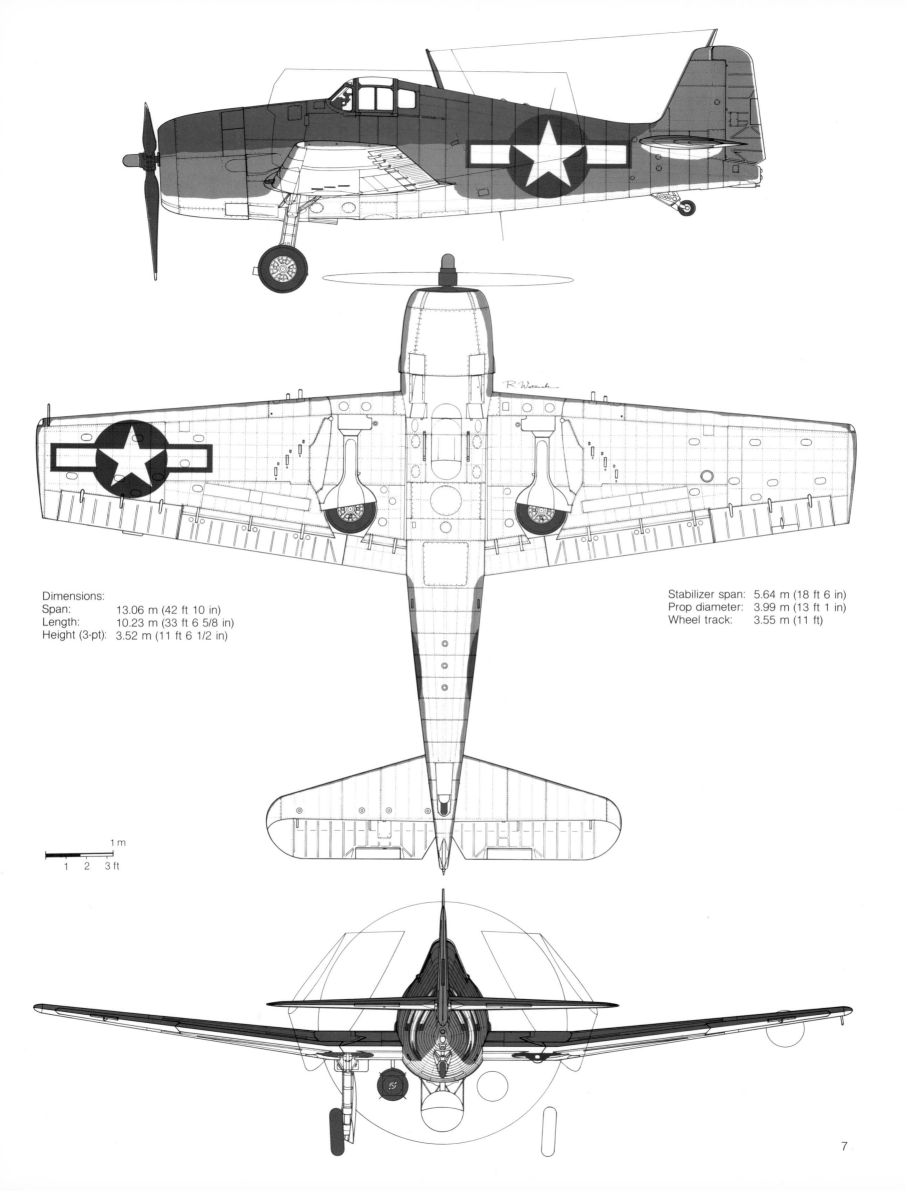

Dimensions:
Span: 13.06 m (42 ft 10 in)
Length: 10.23 m (33 ft 6 5/8 in)
Height (3-pt): 3.52 m (11 ft 6 1/2 in)

Stabilizer span: 5.64 m (18 ft 6 in)
Prop diameter: 3.99 m (13 ft 1 in)
Wheel track: 3.55 m (11 ft)

1 m
1   2   3 ft

7

The Hellcat Family

Although six different models of Hellcat were developed by the Grumman Aircraft Engineering Corporation, only two of them reached production status: The F6F-3 and the F6F-5. All of them retained the characteristic Grumman shape: Chunky fuselage lines, moderate aspect ratios on the tail surfaces, a simple tapered wing with squared-off tips. The Hellcat had its own unique shapes, also. The deep cowl with its bottom inlet for the carburetor and cooler air was one trademark of the series. The wing, seen from the front, was another; it had a thick section, and the dihedral began outboard of the root. The wide-treaded landing gear was a third.

But most characteristic were the humpbacked fuselage lines, drawn to give the pilot the best possible visibility forward. He sat high in the fuselage; the dorsal spine sloped down and aft, and the cowling sloped down and forward. When he sat up straight in the cockpit, his eyes were more than ten feet above the ground.

The Hellcat was not elegant, in the sense of a Spitfire, a Zero, or a Mustang. But it had its own kind of rugged beauty, a functional and tough geometry that spoke volumes. There were good reasons for the angular lines. Parts with straight lines are a lot easier and less expensive to build than parts with curves. A flat surface is easier and less costly than one with multiple contours. Elliptical wings are the theoretical aerodynamic ideal; but a set of properly tapered wings with straight leading and trailing edges come fairly close to the ideal and presented fewer production problems.

As early as February, 1938, Grumman designers were carefully studying the installation of a larger engine in the Wildcat series. Design 33 seems to have been the first of the more formal approaches to the problem; it showed the Grumman XF4F-2, the experimental forerunner of the production Wildcat series, modified to install a big – for that day – Wright Aeronautical Corp. R-2600 engine, model unspecified. That same month, Design 33-A appeared, this time modifying the XF4F-3 with an R-2600 engine. In March, another revision: Design 35 called for a single-engined fighter built around an R-2600 engine, still basically the Wildcat, but beginning to close in on the eventual shapes and sizes of the Hellcat.

There was one more intermediate stage on paper: Design 50, an F4F-4 modified by the installation of an R-2600-10 two-stage engine. It was a powerplant that would deliver 1,290 horsepower at 22,000 feet (6700 m) altitude, and it changed the basic contours of the Wildcat out of almost all recognition.

For reference, the Wildcat had a wingspan of 38 feet (11 m 59 cm) and an overall length of 28 ft. 9 ins (8 m 76 cm). Its wing area was 260 square feet (24 m²). Production Wildcats were powered by the reliable Pratt & Whitney R-1830-86 engines, developing 1,200 horsepower for takeoff and 1,100 horsepower at an altitude of 17,800 feet (5420 m).

Design 50 showed a wingspan of 41 ft. 6 in. (12 m 64 cm) that reflected its greater wing area of 290 square feet (27 m²). Its overall length was 31 ft. 4 in. (9 m 55 cm). The

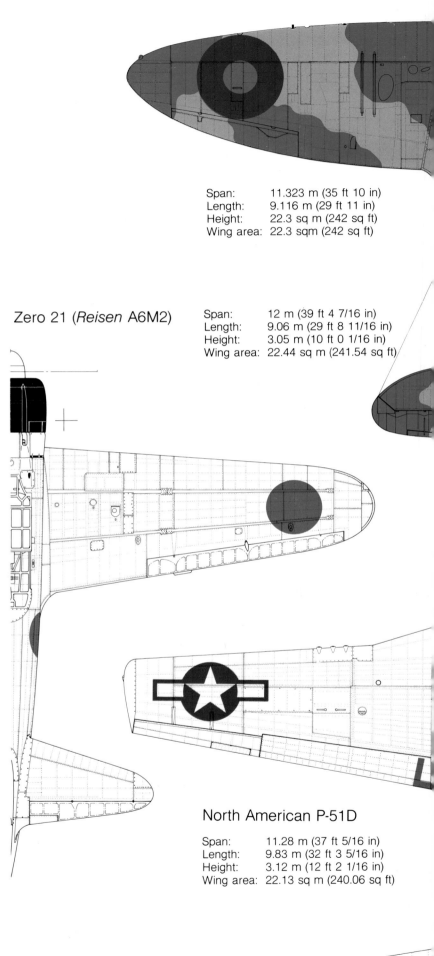

Spitfire MK1a

Span:	11.323 m (35 ft 10 in)
Length:	9.116 m (29 ft 11 in)
Height:	22.3 sq m (242 sq ft)
Wing area:	22.3 sqm (242 sq ft)

Zero 21 (*Reisen* A6M2)

Span:	12 m (39 ft 4 7/16 in)
Length:	9.06 m (29 ft 8 11/16 in)
Height:	3.05 m (10 ft 0 1/16 in)
Wing area:	22.44 sq m (241.54 sq ft)

North American P-51D

Span:	11.28 m (37 ft 5/16 in)
Length:	9.83 m (32 ft 3 5/16 in)
Height:	3.12 m (12 ft 2 1/16 in)
Wing area:	22.13 sq m (240.06 sq ft)

R. Watanabe

R. Watanabe

Pratt & Whitney R-2800 — 10W

These big twin-row, 18-cylinder air-cooled radials were the engines installed on F6F-5 production aircraft. All were equipped with two-stage, two-speed superchargers, and with anti-detonant injection (ADI, or "water injection") systems. The latter generally were removed in the field to reduce weight and eliminate one maintenance headache. The —10W was rated at 2,000 hp. for takeoff, and swung a three-bladed Hamilton Standard Hydromatic propeller of 13 ft. nominal diameter. The powerplant was 52 inches in diameter, and weighed 2,496 pounds in the —10W version. Its displacement, part of its designation, was 2,800 cubic inches. The engine had a reputation for being reliable and rugged; it delivered power when it was needed.

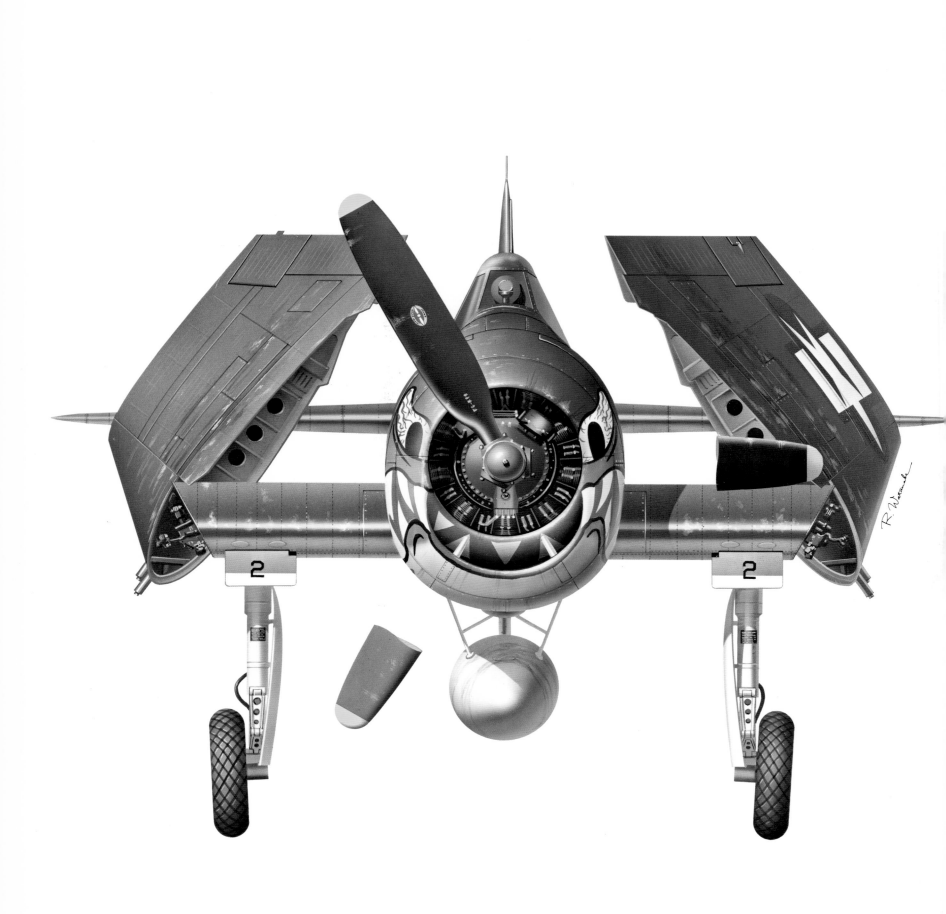

Grumman drawing for the design study – SP56, "B" change – was initialed by Richard Hutton, the brilliant young designer of so many of Grumman's aircraft, on 6 January, 1941. Just nine days later, a draughtsman put the finishing touches on drawing SP-799, "C" change, defining once and for all the final lines of the XF6F-1.

The growth process that had started with more power had produced the Hellcat. The lines that it started with were, by and large, the lines that it finished with. The basic changes to successive models of the Hellcat were minor and none involved any modification that changed the outlines of the F6F in any major way.

The XF6F-1 spanned 42 ft. 10 in. (13 m 6 cm); its overall length was 33 ft. 6¼ in (10 m 21 cm) from the tip of its propeller spinner to the rearmost portion of the tail-fuselage fairing. It stood 11 ft. 6½ in. (3 m 52 cm) high from the three-point static ground level to the highest part of its rearward folding wings.

The folding wing concept was an idea of great simplicity and it has been credited, in Grumman legend, to Roy Grumman's inspired work with a straightened paperclip and a pink gum eraser. Since Grumman legends are, in happy contrast to most, invariably true, that's how the inclined single hinge system was born. It was a brilliant and simple idea, typical of the company's approach to design. It was developed originally for a special version of the Wildcat, and was adapted later to both the Hellcat and the TBF-1 Avenger.

The XF6F-1 received its final definition in Grumman Specification SD-286, and Report No. 2421, dated 24 February, 1941. The Navy awarded the company Contract No. 88263 and the Hellcat was on its way.

Experimental Grumman aircraft were built in a small shop presided over by a resident genius with an occasional temper. He was Julie Holpit, and the craftsmen that worked in his experimental shop were as exceptional as the products of their hands. They were Rodins who worked in sheet aluminium alloys. They knew what to do and how to do it before the first engineering drawing ever hit the shop, and they saved many a young engineer from embarrassment by their skills and their understanding. You got only one chance, though; the second mistake brought a scathing and profane commentary down on your head.

The contract for the XF6F-1 was signed on 30 June, 1941, and on the same day, the Vought XF4U-1 was ordered into production. The coincidence of the dates is important; Vought's Corsair had a head start, but it was a year later getting to the fleet. The Navy had approved the initial design of the Hellcat after running a series of wind-tunnel tests on a one-sixteenth scale model at the Aerodynamical Laboratory. Navy Yard, Washington, DC. The Navy bought two prototypes with that first contract, and specified concurrent testing of the planes.

On 26 June, 1942, the XF6F-1 stood on the ramp at Bethpage, serviced and ready to fly. Its Wright R-2600-16 engine had been run in on the ground, and all of the basic aircraft and engine systems had been checked and rechecked. Bob Hall, who had been responsible for flying the most recent Grumman experimental aircraft, hauled his lanky frame up on the wing and stepped over the sill into the cockpit. He conferred briefly with the plane captain, primed the big Wright powerplant, and started the engine. It coughed into life, jerking and shaking on its mount, spewing exhaust out over the upper surface of the wing.

Hall taxied out, took off uneventfully, and landed after discovering what thousands of Navy pilots were to find out later: the Hellcat was a very fine aircraft, and it flew very well indeed.

But although it flew well, it didn't fly fast enough nor did it climb rapidly enough to meet the requirements the Navy had laid down some months before. Hall's flight tests and their analyses by Grumman aerodynamicists clearly showed the need for more horsepower. Fortunately, there was an engine about to be available, an engine of approximately the same dimensions as the Wright R-2600, but of substantially more horsepower. It had been scheduled for production versions of the Navy's Vought F4U-1 Corsair and the Army's P-47 Thunderbolt; both those planes were delayed, and a production flow of Pratt & Whitney R-2800-10 engines became available. The Navy assigned one to Grumman, and Holpit's men installed it to replace the Wright engine in the XF6F-1, while engineers took notes and sketched. Development programmes moved fast in those days, under the pressures of war and the lesser demands of a simpler era and uncomplicated aircraft. Remember that the first Hellcat-1 prototype had flown 26 June, 1942. On 30 July, Bob Hall clambered into the new XF6F-3, fired up the engine, and made the first test flight of the Pratt and Whitney-powered Hellcat. It lasted less than fifteen minutes, but Hall had found out all he needed to know in that time. Power made the difference and the new Hellcat had it.

On 17 August, though, it didn't have it. The R-2800 quit, and suddenly Hall was flying a very quiet and very heavy glider. He landed it in one of the many farm fields that then covered much of Long Island, Grumman's long-time venue. It wasn't to be the last dead-stick landing in a nearby farmyard for the Hellcat, and this first one, although it did considerable damage to the aircraft and somewhat less to Bob Hall, was taken in stride by both the Navy and Grumman.

The flight tests showed that some minor changes could be made, or needed to be made. The spinner that had covered the propeller hub and delighted the aerodynamicists was an early casualty; nobody else was sorry to see it go. The Curtiss electric propeller, matched to the Wright R-2600 engine, was replaced by one made by Hamilton Standard, a Hydromatic model, matched to the Pratt & Whitney engine.

The production F6F-3s were in the construction phase while the experimental aircrafts were being tested. Grumman's confidence and foresight paid off; the first production Hellcat was ready for its initial flight 3 October, 1942, and from that date there was a constant flow of -3 models rolled out of the Plant 3 doors and parked along the concrete ramps that lined the factory area at Bethpage.

To look ahead of this phase of the story for a moment, the first F6F-3 models were assigned to VF-9 at Naval Air Station (NAS) Oceana. They took them on board the fast carrier USS *Essex* in February, 1943, for carrier qualification

F6F-5, with 1,000 lb (450 kg) bomb.

trials. On 13 March, Hellcats were assigned to the *Essex* Air Group for duty with the fleet, and by the following August they were ready to go into combat. The time between the first flight of the first prototype and the first combat use of the Hellcat totalled 14 months.

The F6F-3 was succeeded in production by the -5 model, an improved version with minor modifications that made it a better fighter and also a better fighter-bomber. The avowed purpose of the Hellcat design had been to fight the Japanese Zeros. It was optimized, as much as it could be, for that task. It had power, speed and the heavy firepower of a sextet of .50-cal machine-guns, and an airframe that could take an unbelievable amount of damage and still fly.

During the combat life of the Hellcat, the proportion of fighters to other types on board carriers steadily increased. In the latter years of the war, fighters predominated; they had been found to be versatile, able to bomb point targets just as well as the Navy's standard dive bombers could. They packed the equivalent of a destroyer broadside in the half-dozen five-inch high-velocity rockets they carried on underwing racks. It was the F6F-5 model that gave the fleet that advantage.

The -5 had a redesigned engine cowling, to help cut down the drag of cooling the mighty R-2800. More power meant more heat, both to the cylinder fins and to the cooling oil, and both demanded increased airflow. To get that without increasing the drag was a neat trick, and the Grumman engineers did it. To drop the drag a few more points, the Navy decided to supplant the paint scheme that had been one of the features of the fleet's aircraft during the middle years of the war. A glossy dark sea blue replaced the three hues of non-specular paint that had contributed its share of skin friction drag to the detriment of Hellcat speed.

The Hellcat's ailerons were redesigned, and a spring tab system was added to reduce the control forces. Grumman spent many hours and dollars during the Hellcat programme trying to come up with a set of ailerons that met the Navy's requirements for the control surfaces, but never succeeded. The spring tab system got them closer than they had been before.

The windshield was cleaned up, and a couple of metal braces were removed for better visibility. The cockpit armour plate was increased somewhat in size, for better protection of the pilot, and the side window behind the cockpit, which had survived in early production units of the -5 model, was removed later in production blocks.

The stabilizer and the fuselage tail structure were strengthened, which meant the heavier-handed Navy pilots could dive the Hellcat faster, and pull out more abruptly, than they had been able to with the -3 model. (It is true that catastrophic failures were almost unknown on the Grumman products of that time. Grumman was often facetiously called "The Iron Works" because of its reputation for building very, very rugged aircraft.)

The Navy made the F6F-5 a fighter-bomber by adding bomb racks to the wing centre section, one on the centreline for ordnance or a droppable fuel tank, and one on each side of the centreline, each capable of holding a 1,000-lb. (450 kg) bomb. The first of the F6F-5 models flew in April, 1944, and they quickly replaced the older -3 aircraft in the fleet.

All together, there were five experimental types of Hellcat and two production models, plus five different sub-types and at least six design studies of other variations on the same theme. The XF6F-1 was the progenitor of the breed. Numerically it was followed by the XF6F-2, although chronologically that specific modification came after the F6F-5 was well into production. The XF6F-2 began as a study for the installation of a special type of turbo-supercharger designed and developed by an expatriate Swiss engineer, Rudolf Birmann. Tests had shown that the supercharger could maintain engine sea-level power to an altitude of at least 40,000 feet (12,200 m), and the promise of such performance was the reason for the design of the XF6F-2. The final engine selection was the Pratt & Whitney R-2800-16; Birmann's Model P14B turbosupercharger was installed for the flight test programme, which began with the first flight of the experimental machine on 7 January, 1944. By July the combination of airframe, engine and turbocharger had shown little significant improvement in standard Hellcat performance, so the programme was stopped, and the XF6F-2 was delivered to the Navy for use in training.

The XF6F-4 was the third stage in the life of the original XF6F-1 prototype. That first experimental Hellcat had then been converted to serve as the -3 prototype; Grumman took it one step further by using it for the -4, a test installation of the Pratt & Whitney R-2800-27, an engine with a single-stage, two-speed built-in supercharger. While it was being converted, the standard armament of six .50-cal machine guns was changed to four 20-mm aircraft cannon, each with 200 rounds of ammunition. The aircraft first flew on 3 October, 1942, and was extensively tested by Grumman and Navy pilots, but was not placed into production. Instead, after the completion of the test programme, it was once again reworked to correspond to a production F6F-3 and was delivered in that state.

Last of the experimental Hellcats was the XF6F-6, powered by the Pratt & Whitney R-2800-18W engine, one of the new "C" type powerplants. Its internal two-stage, two-speed supercharger and water injection for War Emergency Power gave a further boost to the available takeoff and high-altitude military power. That Hellcat first flew 6 July, 1944, as a modified standard production F6F-5 with the XF6F-6 designation. A second XF6F-6 also flew in the test programme, and the results of the increased power were impressive. The Hellcat's top speed was increased substantially, to 417 mph (671 km/h). The Navy had planned to build that high-powered version, but cancelled the programme abruptly on V-J Day, in August, 1945.

Five suffixes were used with Hellcat designations during the life of the aircraft. The first few to carry drop tanks were designated as F6F-3D, but that suffix was soon abandoned as the use of drop tanks became part of the standard configuration. It was later reinstated after the war to indicate aircraft used as drone controllers.

Both the F6F-3 and -5 carried an "E" suffix to indicate that they were equipped with the AN/APS-4 search radar, or an "N" suffix if they were carrying the later AN/APS-6

intercept radar. A number of each production version were built to incorporate camera installations in the fuselage, for post-strike bomb damage assessment; those sub-types carried a "P" suffix.

Postwar, many Hellcats were converted to drone configurations, and were so designated by using a "K" suffix.

The first F6F study to receive a Grumman number after Pearl Harbor was Design 54, the installation of a totally new wing on a standard Hellcat. The wing, of greater area and different geometry, was to have had a low-drag, "laminar flow" airfoil section that had been developed at the National Advisory Committee for Aeronautics' (NACA, the forerunner of today's National Aeronautics and Space Administration) Langley Memorial Aeronautical Laboratory. Work never progressed beyond some drawings, dated February, 1942, and a performance analysis.

Designs 59 and 60 studied the installation of the 28-cylinder R-4360 "Wasp Major" engines in the Hellcat. The two-speed supercharger engine was Design 59: the two-stage engine was Design 60. Both carried a drawing date of August, 1943, and neither went beyond the drawing boards. The reason may have been found in the first analysis of Design 61, cryptically called "F6F with GE unit". The GE unit referred to was the first jet engine in America, and the design was a study of a Hellcat with a mixed powerplant, standard reciprocating radial engine in the nose, and the new General Electric turbo-jet engine in the fuselage with a tailpipe exhausting the jet aft of the Hellcat's rudder. It was a formula that Grumman was to try again and again, and that the Navy experimented with for some years, but it was not a technical success, in any form, and was very soon overtaken by the performance of all-jet aircraft. Last of the identifiable Hellcat studies was Design 69, the installation of the Pratt & Whitney R-2800-22 "C" engine with a two-speed supercharger in what would have been a bomber version of the Hellcat. The two-speed engine developed its power at a lower altitude than a two-stage unit, and so was more suitable for low-level attack and bombing work.

Since the Hellcat could carry bombs, the next logical step was to turn the F6F into a torpedo carrier. This plan was actually carried out but never progressed beyond the test installation

Grumman F6F-5 Hellcat Cutaway

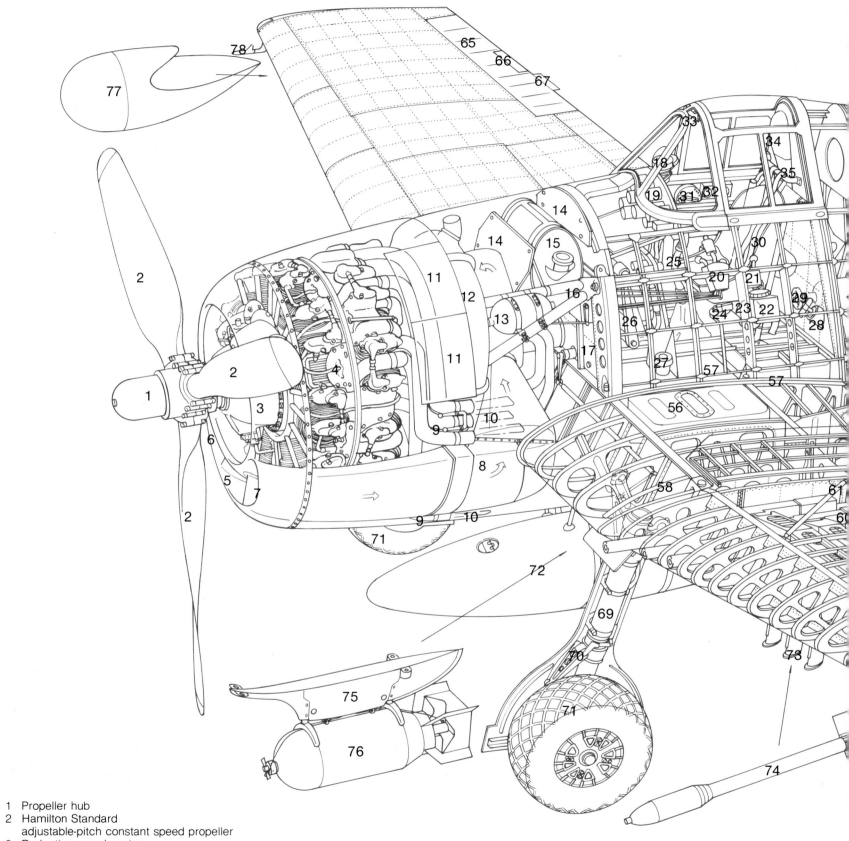

1 Propeller hub
2 Hamilton Standard
  adjustable-pitch constant speed propeller
3 Reduction gear housing
4 Pratt & Whitney R2800-10W twin-row radial air-cooled engine
5 Oil cooler air intake
6 Supercharger air intake
7 Supercharger air intake
8 Supercharger air intake duct
9 Exhaust pipes
10 Exhaust flame damper (F6F-5N only)

11 Cowl flaps
12 Engine carried-on-load mounts with rubber bushing
13 Hydraulic fluid tank
14 Armour plate
15 Engine oil tank
16 Engine mounting frame
17 Main bulkhead

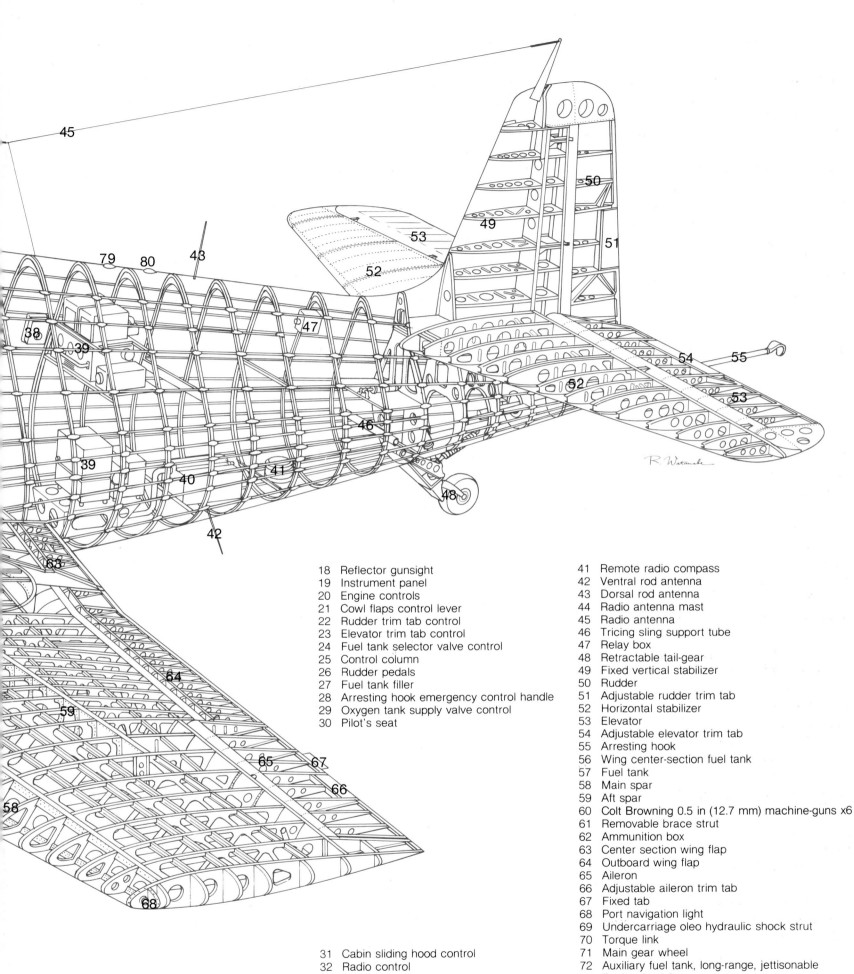

18	Reflector gunsight
19	Instrument panel
20	Engine controls
21	Cowl flaps control lever
22	Rudder trim tab control
23	Elevator trim tab control
24	Fuel tank selector valve control
25	Control column
26	Rudder pedals
27	Fuel tank filler
28	Arresting hook emergency control handle
29	Oxygen tank supply valve control
30	Pilot's seat

31	Cabin sliding hood control
32	Radio control
33	Rear-view mirror
34	Headrest
35	Armour plate
36	Engine water-injection tank
37	Oxygen bottle
38	Junction box
39	Radio equipment
40	Accumulator

41	Remote radio compass
42	Ventral rod antenna
43	Dorsal rod antenna
44	Radio antenna mast
45	Radio antenna
46	Tricing sling support tube
47	Relay box
48	Retractable tail-gear
49	Fixed vertical stabilizer
50	Rudder
51	Adjustable rudder trim tab
52	Horizontal stabilizer
53	Elevator
54	Adjustable elevator trim tab
55	Arresting hook
56	Wing center-section fuel tank
57	Fuel tank
58	Main spar
59	Aft spar
60	Colt Browning 0.5 in (12.7 mm) machine-guns x6
61	Removable brace strut
62	Ammunition box
63	Center section wing flap
64	Outboard wing flap
65	Aileron
66	Adjustable aileron trim tab
67	Fixed tab
68	Port navigation light
69	Undercarriage oleo hydraulic shock strut
70	Torque link
71	Main gear wheel
72	Auxiliary fuel tank, long-range, jettisonable
73	Rocket launcher
74	Rockets, air-ground, 5 in (12.7 cm), x6
75	Bomb launcher
76	Bomb, 1000 lb (454 kg) x1
77	Radar pod (F6F-3N, F6F-5N only)
78	Pitot head
79	Recognition light
80	Section light

In December, 1942, the Navy requested Grumman to study a Hellcat with floats for off-water operations, and the company followed through with tests of a 1/16th scale model at the Navy's Washington wind tunnel. The floats were designed by the Edo Aircraft Co. They were almost 29 feet (8 m 84 cm) long, and each float had a cross-section that was about 40 per cent of the fuselage cross-section area. It would have created a major drag increase and the performance of the Hellcat would have been degraded far too much. The water-borne Hellcat was never developed any further than the wind-tunnel tests and some analyses.

Out of all these prototypes, modifications and design studies, only two standard Hellcats entered production, and they became the backbone of the Navy's fighter strength in the Pacific.

Building the Hellcat

The U.S. Navy accepted its first production Hellcat on 30 September, 1942, and its last on 16 November, 1945. Between those two dates, distanced in time by only 25½ months, Hellcat acceptances totalled 12,275. That's a sustained, average production rate of 481 units each month, a formidable mark for a wartime production effort.

All of those Hellcats were built by Grumman, unlike other Grumman aircraft that were produced and further developed by General Motors. And almost all of them were built in a new plant, erected specifically for the Hellcat. It was built from, among other materials, steel salvaged from New York's Second Avenue Elevated Railway, when that imposing system of mass transit was torn down just before the war.

The angular lines of the Hellcat were chosen to simplify production. Its simple, tapered wing and tail surfaces, its slab-sided fuselage, its internal systems and unseen components were designed, developed and produced by people who, some months before, knew literally nothing about the construction of aircraft and who may never even have seen one up close.

Grumman began its history in a small town on Long Island, New York, at one of the many airports that dotted the chequerboard of flat farmland and villages characteristic of pre-war times. Through successive moves, the company had stayed on the Island, and had drawn its labour force from the area surrounding its plants and airport. That keystone of Grumman policy was one of its great strengths; when the time came to expand production, Grumman was able to call in people from every profession and occupation, to train them to build aircraft and – more importantly – to retain them in that vital task until it had been completed.

The basic Hellcat production programme had its inception in a Navy letter of intent to Grumman, dated 6 August, 1941. The formal contract was signed 23 May, 1942, and by mid-June the first tooling was being built. The first direct labour on the Hellcat had begun, without benefit of production tooling, the previous January.

Leroy R. Grumman, President of what was then called the Grumman Aircraft Engineering Corporation (GAEC), was a quiet, introspective thinker who tended to concentrate on technical problems and to leave the running of the company on a day-to-day basis in the very capable hands of Leon A. Swirbul. Swirbul, who was universally known as "Jake", was an extroverted manager, thoroughly at home with people of all stations in life. His visibility was so high that it frequently seemed as if he, and not Grumman, was the real mover and shaker in the company. No matter; each man was essential, and each was complementary to the other.

But because Jake was always to be seen, moving around the shop floor, greeting visiting Navy pilots, travelling to the Pacific to find out firsthand how Grumman aircraft were holding up, Jake is the one who gets credit for many of the innovative and pioneering aspects of Grumman's approach to production.

The first necessity for Hellcat production was a place to make the aircraft. Grumman's existing facilities were already crowded with lines that were turning out components, assemblies and complete aircraft for the Navy, and for foreign customers. There was no room to sandwich any F6F production among the long aisles that were crowded with Wildcat fuselages, Avenger wings, and even the last of the of J2F-5 "Duck" line.

Accordingly, Plant 3 was designed and built, using – as mentioned – steel from the Second Avenue El. Before the mortar was dry on the brickwork, and before the roof or the fourth wall had been finished, Grumman had moved tools and workers into the plant. It opened officially 1 June, 1942, according to Grumman records; that probably means that the plant was dedicated that day. It is a matter of record that the first production wing panels for the Hellcat were being assembled by stiff-fingered workers during the cold winter months of 1942. The heating plant for the building had yet to be completed; wartime priorities had delayed its delivery, and there was no chance of salvaging something like a heating system from an abandoned factory somewhere. All of the country's industrial base was moving into high gear, and plant space was at an absolute premium.

By the end of 1942, Grumman had delivered ten complete Hellcats; the press releases of the time referred to the quantity as a "full squadron" which was not quite accurate, but forgivable. And from then on, there was no looking back. During 1943, 2,547 Hellcats – a mix of the single XF6F-3/-4 experimental prototype, 2,441 standard F6F-3 Hellcats, and 104 F6F-3N night fighters – were accepted by the Navy. Consider the magnitude of that increase in production: From 10 in one year to 2,547 the very next. To understand that accomplishment a little better, one has to understand the general attitude that prevailed at Grumman among both labour and management.

The population of Long Island was made up of duck farmers, potato farmers, clam-diggers, fishermen and housewives. They became skilled metalsmiths, machinists, crew chiefs, electrical experts, assemblers, inspectors, tool designers, draughtsmen. Grummen recruited, and then trained thousands of personnel during the war years, putting them through programmes that assumed no prior knowledge and that began by telling them what an aircraft was.

More than 30 per cent of the Grumman work force were women, and they proved a point in the war years that still is largely unappreciated: Women can do anything that men can do, and often do it better. They learned as rapidly, and worked as hard. They became any of the hundreds of technicians needed for the efficient production and testing of the Hellcat. Women were aircraft captains, the industrial equivalent of the military crew chief. And some of them became test pilots, lifting the roaring Hellcats off the runway and into the air on acceptance flight tests that demanded much skill and no little bravery.

Grumman pioneered in the introduction of blacks and the credit has been given to Jake for the way it was done. Jake, who knew his shop people, also knew that they felt some hostility to blacks. It was a common social phenomenon in those days. But he knew that they recognized superior performance when they saw it. So Jake recruited a top-level black basketball player, put him through training school, and made him an inspector. He was soon joined by other blacks, picked for their local renown as athletes, and introduced into the work force with no fuss. Within a short time, Grumman workers had accepted the presence of blacks on the assembly lines, in the component shops, and at the lunch tables in the cafeteria. It was a model programme; it resulted in more than 800 blacks employed in the company. And it was accomplished with a minimum of problems.

Among other Grumman innovations was the "Little Green Truck". Wartime priorities made it difficult to keep personal automobiles in good repair, and they frequently broke down on the way to work. A telephone call to the plant brought out "The Little Green Truck", with assistance for the stranded motorist. It was also available to go back to a worker's home and turn the heat off under a forgotten pot roast or to perform some other important errand.

Many of the women workers were the young wives of servicemen, doing their part for the war effort. Many of them had small children at home; so Grumman introduced nursery schools, an industry first. Three were opened in key locations, staffed with full-time nurses, and a consulting pediatrician on call. The schools were open 12 hours a day, and served five meals at different hours to match the mothers' work schedules. The fees that were charged varied, according to the mothers' salaries.

The result of all this was to weld the work force and management closely, and to enable both of them to direct their maximum efforts to the production of aircrafts. Grumman's salary scale was not the highest in the aircraft industry at the time, but the extra benefits were unusual. The company developed an incentive bonus system, to reward workers for goals reached or exceeded. Additionally, there was a bonus for seniority, in effect. The longer one stayed at Grumman, the more that portion of the bonus was. Every Christmas, Grumman, Swirbul and a plant executive lined up in one of the large assembly areas, and handed out bonus cheques and a Christmas turkey to each employee.

It has been called "paternalism"; but most Grumman employees looked on the company's attitude as a good one, and gave their best in return. The semantics were not important.

Five plants contributed to Hellcat production. Plant 1 held the experimental shop, and produced the first prototypes of any Grumman design, including the Hellcats. Plant 3 was where Hellcat production was concentrated, and where components were built and assembled. Plant 11 in Syosset was responsible for building the control surfaces; Plant 13 in Lindenhurst made engine mounts for all the Grumman aircraft; and Plant 14 in Babylon produced the electrical system harness and other wiring for the company.

During 1943, Hellcat production reached its full stride, and by early autumn, Grumman was turning out about 100 F6F-3s every week. The figure continued to climb as the months went by, and by late 1944, Swirbul told the Navy that Grumman was headed for a figure of 700 Hellcats a month. It was more than the Navy could handle; the need did not exist for such a quantity, and they asked Grumman to cut back production to no more than 600 fighters every month.

The peak was reached in March, 1945; Grumman produced 664 aircraft of all types during those 31 days, and of the total, 605 were Hellcats.

The Navy had high praise for the Grumman production effort. James Forrestal, then the Secretary of the Navy, wrote:

"I think everyone has heard of your Hellcats and of the reputation you achieved in 1943 when you set an all-time record in the aviation industry for accelerating production. I have no doubt that you would still be beating your own record month after month if the Navy had not had to slow you down a little."

The Navy also was on record with a statement that Grumman produced more pounds of airframe per taxpayer dollar than any other company in the fighter business. To give dimension to that general statement, the Hellcat's original contract price was $50,000, exclusive of what was then known as GFE: Government Furnished Equipment. By the end of the production run, the price had been cut to $35,000, a 30 per cent reduction in cost to the government. Grumman also liked to point out that the Hellcat was delivered to the Navy for 2/3 of the price of the Vought F4U "Corsair" series.

So the "embattled farmers" – their own description – established production records that set marks for the industry. During the last years of the war, rivalry was intense between Grumman and North American Aviation, then in full production of the elegant P-51 Mustang series. Monthly production rates of the two fighters were posted on bulletin boards, broadcast over the public address system and discussed at lunch. And when, in March, 1945, Grumman set the mark that soundly beat NAA's deliveries for that month, it was announced over the loudspeakers in every factory by Jake Swirbul himself, and it produced a small pandemonium among the workers.

Production was not the only mark that was beaten by the Grumman work force. Absenteeism and turnover were two of the most bothersome factors in the aircraft industry, which has long been noted for having a population of "gipsies'' who move with the contracts. Grumman again was the exception; its unavoidable absenteeism figures were consistently under one per cent during the war, and its annual turnover rate was about three per cent, including those men who were drafted to serve in the armed forces. Those two numbers beat all aircraft industry figures by a substantial margin.

Tested before the Battle

XF6F-2

(David A. Anderton)

Flight-testing has been, and always will be, a vital part of any aircraft development programme. It first seeks to establish the basic safety of the aircraft under test; the early steps explore level flight, simple manœuvres, approaches to the stall, low-speed handling, and other aspects of getting the craft off the ground, into the air, and back down again safely. Subsequent test flights extend those manœuvres, increase the speed and altitude range, perform more abrupt turns. Gradually the entire flight envelope – the aerodynamic and structural limits that completely define the extremes of performance – is explored and the aircraft is judged as safe for other pilots to fly.

Flight-testing is a requirement in any aircraft development programme, because it alone can prove that the operating parameters are what the designers say they are.

The Hellcat flight test programme started when Bob Hall made the first flight on the experimental XF6F-1 and was generally satisfied with what he found. Hall's long experience as a pilot, coupled with his technical and design background, fitted him for the job of initial evaluation of the Hellcat. Later test flying was done by Seldon Converse and, still later, other Grumman test pilots were brought into the programme.

The Navy, as the interested purchaser, also evaluated the Hellcat. Navy pilots flew the aircraft at Bethpage and at the Naval Air Station at Anacostia, Maryland, home of much of the Navy's wartime flight-test activity. And later, when the British bought Hellcats, Royal Navy pilots took F6Fs into the air on a series of detailed test and evaluation missions to see that the planes met the standards the Fleet Air Arm had established.

Finally late in the war and too late to have much influence on Hellcat design, the fighter was tested by NACA pilots at the Langley Memorial Aeronautical Laboratory. Their approach was much more academic and research-oriented; their major concern was with understanding the qualities of flight, and trying to define them for future generations of test pilots.

In the early war days, the popular concept of a test pilot was drawn from the movies: Handsome devil-may-care types who casually risked their lives in screaming power dives and pullouts. Occasionally something went wrong, and then there was an opportunity for some really dramatic moments while the test pilot tried to free himself and parachute to safety.   The image was based on some fact, of course. Part of every flight-test programme was a series of pullouts, entered at high speed. Those manoeuvres are severe tests of the structure of an aircraft, and also of its pilot, because they call for imposing ''G'' loads several times the normal force of gravity.   Grumman's contract with the Navy specified that the company was to demonstrate one aircraft. That meant that it was up to Grumman to show the Navy, through a series of flight tests, that the Hellcat had been designed so that it met the Navy's requirements for flight performance, structural strength and operational flexibility. The preliminary flying was done at the Bethpage plant; for the serious work, the programme moved to the Naval Air Station at Anacostia, down the Potomac River from Washington.

The aircraft chosen for demonstration flying was Bureau No. 04775, the first production F6F-3. The flying at Anacostia began in March, 1943, and proceeded without a hitch until the scheduled dives and pullouts. On the fourth and fifth dives, the horizontal stabilizer was overstressed. It distorted, and cracked, and neither was acceptable in an aircraft designed for the rigours of combat. That ended the demonstration, while the Grumman engineering team went back to report the details of the problem and to ask for a fast solution. Parallel to the piloted flights of the Hellcat, a radio-controlled, pilotless Hellcat was being tested in a series of high-speed dives called Project Fox. The work was done at the Naval Air Station at Cherry Point, South Carolina, and the purpose was to determine whether or not the Hellcat would hold together at speeds greater than the restricted limits that had been imposed on the plane. There were then '' . . . grave doubts about the control characteristics . . .'' in a high-speed dive. Pilots had reported earlier that, in their dives to a Mach number of 0.67 maximum, they had the feeling that a loss of control was imminent.

The radio-controlled dives were begun from 27,000 feet (8230 m); the Hellcat was put into a 70-degree dive, measured from the horizontal, and was allowed to accelerate under full power to an altitude of 10,000 feet (3050 m), where the pullout signal was given by one of the two Grumman Wildcat fighters that controlled the tests. There are reports that one of the dives exceeded 500-mph (805 km/h).

The stabilizer failure took a long time to analyse and fix. Grumman's standard procedure was to strengthen something first and test it again, repeating that cycle until a fix had been achieved. Later, if there were time and reason to do so, the engineers would attempt to analyse what went wrong and why. Remember that this was during a war, and quick fixes, with analyses afterwards, were the rule.

The failure first occurred in an 8G pullout from a dive at 276 mph (444 km/h) indicated airspeed. Subsequent failures happened at higher speeds, in the range of 270 to 390 mph (435 to 628 km/h) indicated, and at load factors above 6.8G. The flow field around the aircraft produced a forced vibration at 3,600 cycles per minute at the tail; that high-speed shake plus the stress of the pullout produced permanent buckling and failure of the skin on the leading edge of the horizontal stabilizer.

In June, 1943, the Navy began a series of static tests on a horizontal tail at the Naval Aircraft Factory, Philadelphia, in an attempt to analyse what was causing the problem. Meantime, the Hellcat was restricted from high-G, high-speed pullouts until the problem was cleared up to the satisfaction of the Navy and company.

Grumman test pilot Corwin H. Meyer, who flew the structural demonstration tests of the Hellcat, remembers what was happening. "The Hellcat was the first Grumman airplane, to my knowledge, that hit the buffet boundary. It was a fairly new phenomenon then, and the first thought was that it was some sort of tail flutter that was causing the trouble with the stabilizer. But somebody in the aerodynamics department came up with the idea that maybe it was the wing wake that was creating the problems with the tail. So we stuck a bunch of long yarns on the wing, long enough to almost reach the tail, and I went up to pull some G. Sure enough, at high speed and just above 6G, those yarns were pointing straight at the horizontal tail. It was the wing wake that was producing the buffeting and the problem.

"After we got past that, we had a very, very fine aircraft, an old man's aircraft. It flew itself off and onto the runway. The cockpit was well-organized, and you could see – really see well – out of the canopy and windshield. I could see the runway ahead of me on the flareout; you couldn't say that about any other fighter, Army or Navy, at that time.

"It was stable laterally, and gusts and crosswinds were no problem. The stall was great. My only complaint – and it was shared by every test pilot who flew the aircraft, whether he was Navy, British or NACA – was that the ailerons were heavy. It seemed to me that we spent most of our flight-test time trying to improve the ailerons to get them to do what the Navy wanted. But nothing seemed to help. The F6 had high lateral damping, and we were working against that."

"Corky" Meyer started his flight-test experience with the Hellcat series with a few flights in the XF6F-1 and the XF6F-3, and did all the structural and powerplant test flights and most of the aerodynamic tests on the production F6F-3 and -5 models. He also flew the sixth production F6F-3 (BuNo. 04780) from its first to last test flight. That machine, like any other aircraft in Grumman's test programme, was called a "dog ship"; the origins of the name are lost in time.

"I flew the 'dog ship' on an altitude test," Meyer remembers, "And when I got to 32,600 feet (9930 m) the engine quit just as suddenly as if it had been turned off. So I glided down, and got the engine restarted at about 7,000 feet (2130 m). I phoned Carl Bellinger (a Republic Aviation test pilot with long experience on the P-47 and its similar powerplant) and talked it over with him, and he told me about the pressurized ignition harness they had on the P-47s. Pratt & Whitney had orders to deliver all their production to Republic, so we got the Navy to lean on them through the

proper channels, and six weeks later we got a harness for our own work. On the first flight with the pressurized ignition system, I got up to 37,000 feet (11300 m) with no problem."

Meyer emphasized the strength of the Hellcat: "You could still pull 3G at 420 knots, and about all you could stand at the low-speed end of the envelope. The Dash 3 had a 6.5G limit, and the Dash 5 let you go to 7.5G. And about there the average pilot is beginning to feel the strain a bit.

"The landing gear was one of the more rugged features of a very rugged aircraft. The Navy requirements called for a six-foot free drop with the aircraft at landing weight. But the 'Schwendler factor' came in here again; Grumman kept on going after making the six-foot (1.8 m) drop successfully, and took it up to ten feet (3 m). They couldn't go any higher, because the canopy was practically up against the ceiling in the test building."

NACA pilots made a series of 30 flights in the second production F6F-3 (Bu. No. 04776), beginning in February, 1944, and ending 15 May. They reported, in NACA Memorandum Report L5B13, that " . . . pilots were favourably impressed with the longitudinal stability and control of the F6F-3 aircraft. They considered it an easy airplane to fly. The control forces in abrupt and steady manoeuvers were satisfactory. Also, the airplane was very easy to land."

But the NACA research pilots noted some problems, including the fact that the aileron control characteristics did not completely fill either Navy or NACA minimum requirements. There was objectionable rudder shake in all flight conditions, and it occurred right through the speed range. The least stable condition tested was one that was going to cause some problems in carrier operations: The wave-off. And they noted that the Hellcat was difficult to control in highspeed flight.

The thorough NACA analysis of the Hellcat's stall characteristics reported that "Stall warnings existed in steady flight for glide, climb and landing conditions in the form of increased vibration, a duct howl in power-off conditions, and gentle buffeting." That buffeting only happened if the approach to the stall was made very slowly and deliberately; otherwise it was not among the warnings. And there was no warning of stall in either the approach or wave-off conditions, further aggravating that latter manoeuver. The NACA tests confirmed Meyer's opinion of the stall: " . . . roll-off was mild, checked easily by ailerons and rudder."

The Navy's Board of Inspection and Survey made its final performance flight tests of the F6F-3 over the better part of a year, between August, 1944, and June, 1945. There were four basic items that had been guaranteed by Grumman in the contract; Grumman met two of them, and nearly made the other two. Maximum speed had been guaranteed to be greater than 377 mph (607 km/h), using military power at 23,400 feet (7130 m); the Hellcat under test did 376 mph (605 km/h). Its stalling speed, power off, at sea level, had been guaranteed to be less than 80.6 mph (129.7 km/h); the actual number in the Navy tests was 81.5 mph (131.2 km/h).

The company had said that the service ceiling – that altitude where the rate of climb is 100 feet (30 m) per minute – would exceed 38,000 feet (11580 m), and the Navy

A formation of F6Fs over Guam.

achieved 38,100 feet (11610 m). Finally, the takeoff distance in a 25-knot wind, a critical factor in carrier-based operations, had been promised to be less than 285 feet (87 m) by Grumman. The Navy got its test Hellcat off the deck in 265 feet (80 m).

By then, of course, Navy pilots by the hundreds had flown the Hellcats off carrier decks, had fought with them from sea level to the thin blue edge of the stratosphere, had jammed the throttles forward for all the power they could get, and had manoeuvered abruptly, violently, recklessly, in their fights with the Japanese aircraft. The flight-test reports, if they knew about them, were of no interest whatever except as they imposed limitations that were clearly stated in large capital letters in their pilots' handbooks.

Those limitations were few. When diving the F6F-3 or -3N, do not exceed 415 knots IAS below 10,000 feet (3000 m); for most of the -5 and -5N models, do not exceed 440 knots. Maximum permissible speed for unlimited use of the ailerons is 260 knots IAS (Indicated Air Speed). Don't exceed +5G and −2G limits of acceleration. Don't lower the landing gear above 135 knots, or it will trail and not lock down. (Pilots later took advantage of that to dive-bomb with the landing gear trailing to act as an air brake.)

But there was one limitation on the Hellcat that did not appear in the handbooks. It was taught in training for combat, and it was repeated and repeated at every level by instructors, flight leaders, squadron commanders, air group commanders, and probably task force admirals. It was simple: Don't dogfight with a Zero.

And even so, it was a lesson that had to be learned again and again in combat. Some of those who learned were lucky and escaped, to fight again. But those who ignored that advice and tried to stay with the Zero in its agile aerobatics too often died.

Combat, in the final analysis, was the ultimate set of limitations imposed on the Hellcat.

Hellcat's First Fight

"BULLETIN: Washington, DC, Oct. 12 (Delayed) – Grumman Hellcats shot down 21 Japanese planes with a loss of only two in an air battle over an unidentified South Pacific island, the Navy disclosed today. The raid was the Hellcats' first appearance in combat.

"A special Navy bulletin also announced that Hellcats at Wake Island on October 5 and 6 accounted for 61 Jap planes without the loss of a single Grumman fighter.

"It is presumed that the delayed Navy announcement regarding the 21 –2 victory in the South Pacific refers to a battle which took place before the September 3 raid on Marcus Island. The score for the two battles – that one and the Wake Island action – now stands at 82 – 2 in favor of the Grumman fighters."

That news dispatch, reprinted in *Plane News*, the Grumman plant newspaper, for 14 October, 1943, was greeted with wild enthusiasm in Plant 3, where the Hellcats were being produced. Like many other wartime reports on both sides, that one contained its exaggerations, and later, more detailed analysis of the battles reduced the claims somewhat. But the basic truth was there: The Hellcats had been in their first combat, and had acquitted themselves outstandingly.

It was quite different from the news of the initial combat of the Grumman TBF-1 Avenger. Six of the then-new torpedo bombers, based on Midway Island as part of Torpedo Squadron 8, attacked the Japanese fleet early on the morning of 4 June, 1942. Five had been shot down and the sixth just managed to get back, badly damaged and with a dead rear gunner.

Zero 22 of the Tainan *Kokutai* on its way from the Rabaul airbase to attack Guadalcanal, 11 October, 1942.

The Battle of Midway was a turning point in the war. From then on, the power of America's sea and air forces was to grow rapidly, to overwhelm the Japanese. The U.S. Navy had a single fleet carrier left at the end of 1942; but in little more than one year, it had added eight *Essex*-class fast carriers, each with a 90-aircraft air group, nine *Independence*-class carriers, each with a 35-aircraft group, and 25 escort carriers.

Further, there was a new generation of Naval aircraft entering service. The Avenger was rapidly replacing the aged Douglas Devastator; Curtiss SB2C Helldiver bombers promised much better performance than the Douglas Dauntless they were supplanting – a promise, incidentally, that was a long time in the keeping – and the Hellcat was taking over from the Wildcat as the first-line fighter.

The first combat-ready batch of Hellcats was assigned to Fighting Squadron Nine (VF-9, in Navy shorthand) and they learned how to handle the new planes at NAS Oceana. The squadron boarded the *Essex*, in February, 1943, for carrier qualification trials to prove out both the aircraft and the pilots. The squadron was officially assigned to the *Essex* on 13 March, 1943, and declared ready for combat. The time and place had yet to be chosen.

The Pacific was about to become the stage for a massive, island-hopping series of assaults that were to roll the Japanese garrisons back, one by one, either by defeat or by bypassing them. Amphibious task forces, supported by massive Naval – and frequently Army Air Forces – air strength, were assembling and provisioning for the battles that lay ahead. The tactical plan was similar for each: A saturation bombardment of the Japanese defences by Navy dive-bombers and fighter-bombers, supported in strength by covering fighters and by shelling by off-shore battleships, cruisers and destroyers. After this softening of the defenders, the Marines would storm the beaches, establish a beachhead, and

fight their way inland until the Japanese surrendered or were slaughtered.

The envisioned role of the Hellcat in these battles was a dual one. It was responsible for maintaining combat air patrol above its carriers and the fleet, knocking down any Japanese aircraft that attempted to attack the ships. It was also responsible for ground attack, bombing and strafing the Japanese positions ahead of the invading Marines, and working with Marine fighters that were giving close support to the Leathernecks on the ground.

A dress rehearsal was to be a strike against Marcus Island, a lone mountain top lying about halfway between Wake Island and the Japanese Bonin Islands. Marcus had been hit earlier by Navy bombers in March, 1942, but the damage they did then was light and ineffective militarily. The second Marcus strike was scheduled for 31 August, 1943, and the Navy sent Task Force 15 against it. TF15, commanded by Rear Admiral Charles A. Pownall, was built around two fast carriers, the *Essex* and the *Yorktown*, plus the light carrier *Independence*.

TF15 sailed from its Hawaiian rendezvous on 23 August, headed on a course to bypass Marcus to the northwest. The plan was to turn south and hit the northern side of the base, expected to be the weaker sector of the defences. Primary target was the Japanese airfield and its aircraft, rumoured to be a fairly large air unit.

The two carriers launched their aircraft in darkness, because the tactical plan called for strikes against the airfield no later than one hour after dawn. Both "Fighting Nine", from the *Essex*, and "Fighting Five" from the *Yorktown*, dispatched their Hellcats as part of the first strike. Commander James H. Flatley, CAG (Commander, Air Group) aboard the *Yorktown*, made the last takeoff from that carrier. His job that day was to be air boss to direct the strike from his Hellcat. Because he was expected to stay on the scene for the duration

A photographic F6F-5P on the deck of the *Bunker Hill* being readied for missions over Iwo Jima, 19 February, 1945. *(National Archives)*

Fighting Nine, from the *Essex* (CV-9), takes off for an attack on Truk on 16 February, 1944. *(National Archives)*

of the fight, his plane was carrying a pair of auxiliary fuel tanks. Flatley later wrote this description of the engagement; it appeared in *Plane News* on 16 September, 1943.

"A Grumman 'Avenger' was the first plane over Marcus at 6:08 a.m. The pilot found a bright light burning in the air base's control tower, so he turned on his own running lights so that any watching Japs might think his plane was one of their own. Then he dropped his bombs from low altitude and was away before the anti-aircraft woke up.

"The island was immediately lighted by fires as the heavy bombs exploded. At the same time the supporting fighters began their strafing.

"The anti-aircraft opened up after about three minutes. Meanwhile the fighters in the light of the fires saw seven Mitsubishi bombers beautifully parked in a line on the runway. Four Hellcats immediately commenced low-altitude strafing runs through heavy ack-ack. They made repeated passes dodging over the targets in a series of wingovers and destroyed the seven bombers one by one. They finished the job in ten minutes. It was a beautiful job and the highlight of the day . . . Incidentally, this is the first time I know of that carrier fighters have done night strafing."

The Japanese were taken by surprise, and were unable to get any defending aircraft into the air. Only the anti-aircraft gunners were able to fight back, and their firing downed two Hellcats and a TBF. The Hellcats assigned to combat air patrol over the island orbited with nothing to do, and watched the fight develop below them. The F6Fs from Fighting Five and Nine continued to strafe the field, working over the anti-aircraft battery positions to draw their attention away from the slower dive bombers that were hitting the buildings and potholing the runways.

The task force launched nine strikes against Marcus Island that day, and by late in the afternoon all Japanese defensive activity had ground to a halt. The last sporadic firing of the anti-aircraft guns stopped, and left the Navy in complete possession of the skies above Marcus. It was an early, and classical, example of the gaining of air superiority, and the importance of that superiority in determining the way the rest of the battle would go. It was a demonstration that the U.S. Navy would repeat, time after time, as it advanced inexorably across the broad reach of the Pacific.

The combat debut of the Hellcats in the Marcus strike triggered a long-lasting argument about which squadron first flew the planes into battle. Recently, Barrett Tillman, a careful researcher and fine writer, set the record straight for that day at Marcus Island. He pointed out that Fighting Five launched first, and could rightfully be credited with first going into battle with the Hellcats. But Fighting Nine, a few minutes later to launch, diverted two of its Hellcats on the way to the primary targets at Marcus to strafe a pair of Japanese picket boats. So VF-9 gets credit for the first shots fired in anger by Hellcats. Among the things that plague historians are the difficulties of proving, once and for all, any particular "first". The case of the Hellcat's first combat is one of those specific examples.

On 5 October, 1943, Lt. (JG) H. A. Cantrell, of Fighting Squadron 33 ("Hellcats"), wrote a letter to his brother:

"Our squadron was the first one in action with this new plane and not that squadron that made a raid on the Marcus Island.

"While we were in action we made a good record. I can't tell you how many planes our squadron shot down, but it was quite a few. I only got credit for half a Zero. My division leader and I shot down one together. One other day our division of four were jumped by eight Zeros. We went into our weave [The so-called 'Thach weave', a mutually supporting attack maneuvre developed by Cdr. James Thach while flying 'Wildcats'] and that was the only thing that saved us. I am sure that I got one of them that day but it wasn't confirmed. I could see part of his plane fly over my wing and my division leader saw two splashes but didn't actually see the plane hit the water."

Now, almost 40 years later, the details fade from memories. Records were often poorly kept in the pressure of daily combat, and we may never know exactly which squadron, let alone which pilot, first took the Hellcat off on a combat mission, first fired the guns in anger, first scored a victory over a Japanese aircraft. One fact remains. The Hellcat entered combat early in the autumn of 1943 and, from then on, the dimensions of air war in the Pacific changed. The Navy had a fighter that could gain control of the skies over the battleground.

Hellcat Actions and Aces

Neither the Japanese nor the Americans were able to gain a decisive advantage during early air combat in the Pacific. Neither country had an overwhelming quantity of skilled pilots available and neither held the technological edge in aircraft design that might have turned the tide of battle.

The development and deployment of the fast carrier force by the U.S. Navy introduced a new – and eventually decisive – factor into naval air power. The task force was mobile airpower, positioned in the Pacific on fast carriers that were supported by the traditional fighting ships. The fast carrier forces – later designated as numbered Task Forces – became the leading edge of the campaigns that were to destroy one Japanese outpost after another and finally reach the Japanese home islands themselves.

The fighter was the key element in the development of the tactics used by the task force. Fighter primary missions were seen first as combat air patrol, to defend their carriers, and second as escort, to defend the dive-bombers and torpedo planes set out on strikes. But the fighter soon proved itself to be a versatile and rugged weapons platform that could launch rockets or drop bombs with precision.

It was a stroke of good fortune, because as the war progressed, the other major elements of the air strike force did not measure up to their expected potential. The Douglas Dauntless dive-bombers were supposed to be replaced in fleet service by the greatly improved Curtiss Helldiver, but that latter aircraft was long delayed in reaching the fleet. When it did arrive, it was not greatly admired; it was quickly nicknamed "The Beast". The role of the torpedo bomber diminished steadily during the war. It was a high-risk way to attack shipping, and torpedo designers had not produced a

The F6F-5 is about to leave on a fighter sweep over Northern Luzon province in the Philippines, part of the Task Force 38 assault before the scheduled invasion by MacArthur's forces.

The humidity of this October, 1944, day condenses behind the propeller tips and is visible as vapor trails corkscrewing aft in the slipstream.

(National Archives)

dependable weapon that could be counted upon to run true and detonate after the drop from an aircraft.

Although it was not recognized at the time, the Navy was very dependent on the performance and the versatility of the Hellcat. And the F6F itself was unproven in long and continuing combat.

The strike against Rabaul on 5 November, 1943, was the first major air battle for Hellcats of the fast carrier force. It was, in a way, a test of the concept itself. Rabaul's harbour was the anchorage for a large number of Japanese merchant ships and warships; the latter were a potential threat to the thinly spread fighting ships of the U.S. Navy, just beginning their long advance across the Pacific. A clutch of cruisers lay at anchor and the mission of the Navy's Task Force 38 was simple: Get in, get the cruisers, get out.

Rabaul was heavily defended by anti-aircraft and fighters; at least 50 Zeros were routinely available as top cover for the base. Supplementing the ground-based anti-aircraft batteries would be the guns of the cruisers and any other warships in the harbour.

Toward this bastion sailed TF38, built around the 16-year old *Saratoga*, and the eight-month old *Princeton*. They launched their aircraft more than 200 miles (320 km) to the southeast of Rabaul, under rain clouds and an overcast sky. All available aircraft went; the striking force was a mix of about two dozen each of SBDs and TBFs, escorted by 52 Hellcats. Sixteen of them, from Fighting Twelve aboard the *Saratoga*, flew about 1,000 (305 m) feet above the bombers; in the lead fighter was VF-12's skipper, Cdr. Joseph C. Clifton. VF-12's executive officer, Lt. Cdr. R. G. Dose, led another 16 F6Fs stepped 3,000 feet (914 m) above Clifton's group. Well above both formations were the Hellcats from VF-23, off the *Princeton*, led by Cdr. Henry L. Miller. The air boss for the battle was the Air Group Commander, Cdr. Howard H. Caldwell, flying a TBF escorted by one Hellcat from the *Sara* and one from the *Princeton*.

Japanese radar had picked up the strike force and the Zeros were already in the air when the lead pilots sighted Rabaul. Their orders were to go straight to the target and to stick together for that run. The fighters were to fly escort, and not to be enticed away to tackle the three-plane flights of Zeros. Protection of the bombers was the primary mission.

The bombers ploughed into the heavy flak and drove straight through to their targets. The Zeros, unwilling to enter their own flak zones, hung around the edges until the bombing was over and the planes were leaving the area. And then the fight erupted. And, as "Jumping Joe" Clifton said later: "The F6F proved to be far and away the best fighter in the air . . . definitely faster at sea level than the Zeke . . . did not have the maneuverability or the climb advantage, but again the Thach weave plus the rugged construction and pilot protection offset these . . . The F6F's superior diving speed proved a Godsend in places where weaving was impossible."

The cruisers were hit and three were heavily damaged. Five Hellcats and five bombers were lost; the U.S. pilots claimed 11 Japanese planes shot down and 14 more probably shot down. Those claims were exaggerated, like most of the air combat claims made during the war. But the important point had been made. The Hellcat had shown its abilities within the framework of a difficult mission and the melee that followed. The Rabaul strike was the real baptism of fire for the F6F. Within a few days, Rabaul was hit again; and then the campaign against the Gilbert Islands, led by Task Force 50 re-emphasized the Hellcat's capability. In that latter campaign, the F6F came into its own, and established, once and for all, its superiority over anything the Japanese could put into the air. After the Gilberts, came assaults on the Marshalls. On 29 January, 1944, Rear Admiral Marc Mitscher opened the fight to take Kwajalein with a strike by about 700 carrier-based aircraft. Mitscher, commanding Task Force 58 with its 15 heavy battleships, 18 cruisers, about 100 destroyers and a mix of 17 carriers of heavy, light and escort types, directed "Operation Flintlock", the beginning of the end for Japan.

Kwajalein was followed by the occupation of the Marshall Islands, strikes on the Western Caroline Islands, landings at Hollandia in New Guinea and the assault against the Marianas Islands, slated to become the bases for the gigantic Boeing B-29 Superfortress long-range bombers that were to destroy Japanese industries, armaments and cities.

There was however an unusual Hellcat action far removed from the Pacific during mid-1944. Said a Navy dispatch in August, 1944:

"New Hellcats piled up an impressive record of destruction during landings in Southern France. Based on baby flattops, the F6F-5s gave close support to the U.S. Army troops and blasted the Nazis along the shore during their northward retreat."

Two U.S. Navy carriers – the *Kasaan Bay* and the *Tulagi* – supported that landing with Hellcats. In their fighter-bomber role, they first struck the beaches before the landing of the amphibious assault force, then spotted shell bursts for the off-shore naval artillery firing. After that, they chased retreating German columns. VFO-1, flying off the *Tulagi*, claimed to have shot up 487 motorized transports and other vehicles.

On 19 August, a pair of Hellcats shot down three Luftwaffe Heinkel 111s, caught near Lyon, France; another F6F duo searching for a fight found and shot down three Junkers Ju 52 transports.

The reputation of the "Grumman Iron Works" was upheld time and again in combat. One Hellcat of VF-5 aboard the *Yorktown* came back from a raid against Palau and grazed a gun turret after a shaky landing. The plane continued up the deck, shedding its wing, then its empennage, then finally its after fuselage up to the armour plate bulkhead behind the pilot. Ensign Black threw back the canopy and climbed out of the ruins, his only injury a forehead scratch.

Normal landings incorporated post-flight checks while the plane was still in motion. Once the Hellcats picked up the arresting gear wires, they were quickly brought to a halt while the "airedales", the plane crews on the carrier deck, disengaged the wire and gave the taxi signal. When the pilot passed the bridge, he held up his open hand with fingers tallying his victories. As he passed the radioman on deck, that

'Hangar Queen,' a Hellcat grounded several times in one week for minor repairs, is about to be launched on a mission to Sakashima.   (Marine Corps)

specialist would tap his ear, asking the pilot if the radio worked properly. Finally the Hellcat was spotted forward on the deck and the wheels were chocked. The engineering officer then moved toward the plane, holding up his thumb. If the pilot answered with the same gesture, he knew the plane was mechanically OK. If not, he waited for the pilot to climb down and start the list of complaints.

The compression of action into the space of a carrier deck made for a few furious minutes during each launch and recovery of aircraft. Not all the landings were good, nor were all of them as fortunate as Ensign Black's escape. One Hellcat came in for a landing on a strange carrier, a common practice when fuel was low after the return from combat. Just as the pilot was about to cut the power, the sea lifted the ship's stern and the F6F slammed onto the deck in a very hard landing. The guns fired a short burst; apparently they had not been safetied. The belly tank broke loose during the arresting and its momentum carried it into the propeller, which sliced it into chunks and sprayed the remaining gasoline over the aircraft. The fire was extinguished, and the pilot only received minor burns. But 11 men on the carrier island were wounded by bullets, and five planes spotted on the forward deck were holed.   Another Hellcat, being respotted with its wings folded, somehow triggered off a burst from the six .50-cal machine-guns. The bullets went right through the flight deck, wounded six men on the hangar deck, and a man in sick bay on the third deck below.

Hellcats flew a classic escort action over Manila in October, 1944, that was a textbook example of that type of mission.

They were from Task Force 38.4, commanded by Rear Admiral Ralph Davison. The fast carrier *Enterprise* was in the group, which was tasked to send its planes against Nelson Field, a Japanese air base on Luzon. The *Enterprise* launched at 0900 on 15 October; its strike force consisted of nine Helldivers and eight Avengers with an escort of 16 Hellcats from "Fighting Twenty" under Cdr. Fred Bakutis. The Helldivers and Avengers were carrying bombs; the Hellcats were armed with rockets in addition to their standard ration of .50-cal ammunition.

The bombers cruised in at 15,000 feet (4570 m), with Hellcats above and to the sides. Bakutis led the top two elements – four Hellcats – at 22,000 feet (6706 m). They were still 40 miles out of Manila Bay when Bakutis saw the Japanese fighters. There were about 40 Oscars, and they knew the first part of their business. They boxed in the bombers and their escorts, cruising along a parallel course, while the Navy pilots watched and waited.

And then, singly, the Oscars began runs against the formation, as feints to attempt to draw off the Hellcats. That didn't work; the F6Fs stayed in formation and refused to break off for battle. The Japanese continued to run in, still singly, and pressed their attacks until they had to be fought. A Hellcat element would swing wide to meet the thrust, and then shoot down the intruder. It was, in retrospect, a very one-sided fight. The Japanese were unable to get through the protective screen, and were shot out of the sky, one at a time, until nearly all of the intercepting force had been destroyed. There were no American losses, either to the heavy flak, or to the fighters. And, said Cdr. A. E. Riera, who was flying the leading Helldiver, "Not one enemy fighter approached within gun range."

By the end of 1944, the fleet was calling its airpower "The Big Blue Blanket". The Hellcats had seized air superiority and, except for an occasional nuisance raider, no Japanese aircraft penetrated the defences to attack the fleet.

Cdr. James S. Thach organized fighter sweeps by day and interdiction strikes by night to seek out and destroy what was left of Japanese air power. On 14 October, the day before the classic escort mission described earlier, Thach's

A Hellcat lands heavily and its six HVAR rockets bounce along the deck of the *Essex*. (National Archives)

Six Aces In The F6F

The complete list of U.S. Navy and Marine Corps aces who achieved their string of five or more victories while flying the Hellcat is far too long for the scope of this book. Dozens of pilots earned the title "ace," some in a single combat sortie. Others made their scores one at a time, over a period of some months in battle.

The six aces named here head the list, and their exploits are a representative cross-section of the ways in which Navy and Marine pilots became aces.

Cdr. David McCampbell, Medal of Honour winner, rolled up a total score of 34 aerial victories and 20 aircraft destroyed on the ground. He commanded Air Group 15 on board the fast carrier *Essex* in strikes against Marcus Island in May, 1944, and later in the attacks against Saipan, the battles of the Philippine Sea and of the Leyte Gulf. On 19 June, 1944, the day of the Great Marianas Turkey Shoot, McCampbell got seven Japanese fighters. On 12 September, over the Philippines, he got four more and the next day shot down three. His best day's shooting was 24 October, when he and his wingman Lt. (jg) Roy W. Rushing of VF-15 attacked a formation of 40 Zeros. In a one-sided slaughter, McCampbell shot down nine while Rushing got six. The fight lasted about ten minutes, and not once did the Japanese attempt to defend themselves or to attack the two Navy pilots.

Second-ranking Hellcat ace was Lt. Eugene A. Valencia, of Fighting Nine aboard the *Essex* during his first combat tour in 1943. He shot down seven Japanese planes during three sorties over Rabaul, Tarawa and Truk. Valencia developed a variation on the Thach weave which used a four-plane section instead of the usual two-plane flight. When he returned to combat in the Pacific in 1945, he tried the new tactic – which was to become known as "Valencia's mowing machine" – in action over Tokyo on 16 February. Valencia himself got six planes on that first time out. By the end of his tour he

sweeps nailed 46 out of 69 Japanese aircraft while they were trying to take off from their home bases to defend them against the marauding Hellcats. Eight F6F-5s from "Fighting Eighty" ran into a formation of 27 Zeros and Oscars moving into the Philippines from Formosa as reinforcements, and proceeded to shoot down 20 of them in a short brawl.

Toward the end of the war, it was almost embarrassingly easy to down Japanese fighters. By then, the Empire had long since lost the training battle; its pilot schools were turning out eager and enthusiastic pilots whose knowledge of the rudiments of air fighting and tactics was very sketchy. There were many instances of Japanese fighter formations that simply held course while they were picked off, one by one, by Hellcats that harrassed them. The best-known of all such one-sided engagements was the "Marianas Turkey Shoot," an air action which is described in the next chapter.

This Hellcat, taking off from the *Hornet* for a strike against Formosa nearly went over, but the pilot made it. (National Archives)

had shot down 16 more, and had made aces out of each of his three wingmen in the section. His final victory tally was 23.

Lagging Valencia by only one victory was Lt. Cecil E. Harris. He'd bagged two Japanese while assigned to a Wildcat Squadron, and got 22 more after joining VF-18 aboard the *Intrepid*. But Harris' unique claim to fame is that, on three separate occasions, he shot down four Japanese aircraft in a day's combat.

Reading anything about Lt. Alexander Vraciu gives one the impression that he liked to fight. His final score, before he was knocked down over the Philippines in December, 1944, totalled 19 aerial victories and 21 destroyed on the ground. Vraciu did two tours; the first was with Fighting Six on the *Independence* and, later, on the *Intrepid*. That tour accounted for nine of the planes that he shot down. The remaining ten victories were achieved while with VF-16 aboard the *Lexington*. The most outstanding of his air combats was over the Marianas; he shot down six Japanese bombers in eight minutes of a fierce fight. He escaped from his aircraft after being knocked out of combat that December, and continued to fight the Japanese as a member of a Philippine guerrilla band until the end of the war.

Lt. Patrick D. Fleming also did two combat tours. His first, with VF-80 on the *Ticonderoga*, netted him ten Japanese planes; his second, as a pilot in VBF-80 on the *Hancock*, accounted for eight more Japanese victories. On the latter tour, he shot down five enemy aircraft in a single combat 16 February, 1945. But since he was already an ace twice over, the feat attracted little attention. Besides, by the end of the war it was not uncommon.

Lt. Cornelius N. Nooy also did that little trick, but he did it the hard way: With a 500-lb. (230 kg) bomb still in the rack on his Hellcat. Nooy, who flew two tours with VF-31 on the *Belleau Wood* got into a fight on 21 September, 1944, with his Hellcat still armed for dive-bombing. He turned to the attack and shot down five Japanese aircraft in the single combat. His final tally was 19 victories.

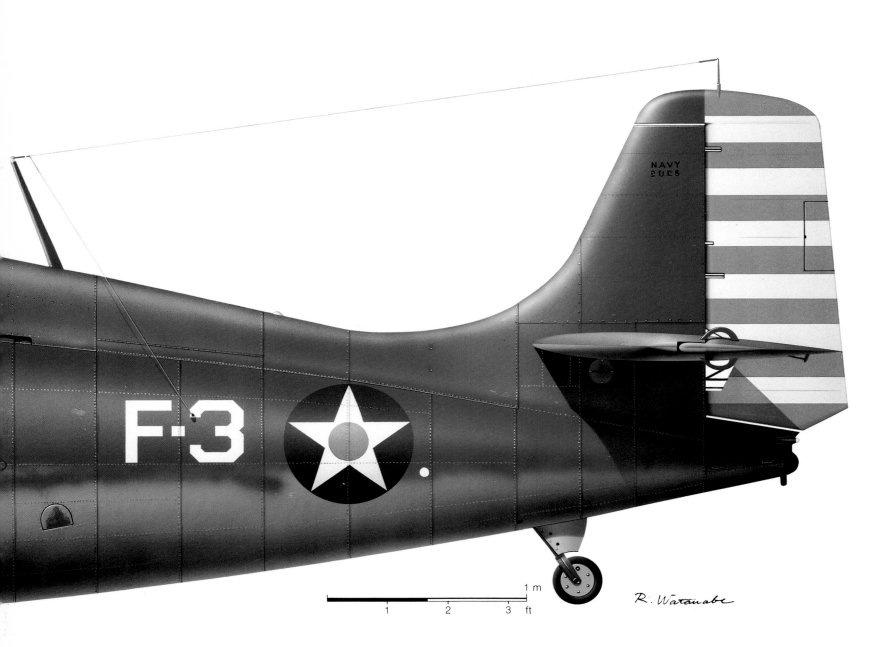

R. Watanabe

Grumman F4F-3 Wildcat

'Felix the Cat' insignia identifies this Wildcat as part of Fighting Squadron Three (VF-3); The row of Japanese flags and the stenciled line below the sliding canopy further mark the airplane as one flown by Lt. Edward H. O'Hare. He was flying combat air patrol 20 February, 1942, when nine twin-engined Mitsubishi G4M1 bombers, out of Rabaul, hurtled down on the task force. *Lexington* had 12 of her VF-3 Wildcats in the air; in the ensuing fight, more were launched and some

were recovered. The Japanese lost five, fast; the remaining four headed for the horizon, with all but two of the Americans in pursuit. From another heading came nine more G4M bombers, now with only Wildcats between them and the *Lexington*. The guns of one F4F jammed; only O'Hare was left to blunt the attack. He sliced into the formation, shot down five in four minutes and scored hits on three others. For that daring feat of arms, O'Hare received the Medal of Honor. Differences persist today about the specific markings of the airplane he flew in that epic combat; he was photographed at another time in F-13.

Grumman F8F-2 Bearcat

The last of a long line of piston-engined fighters that began with tubby biplanes in the 1930s, the Bearcat (Grumman Design 58) was developed as an interceptor, to be based on escort carriers. The small deck and lower speed of those carriers made a short takeoff distance imperative. The Bearcat was optimized around requirements for a

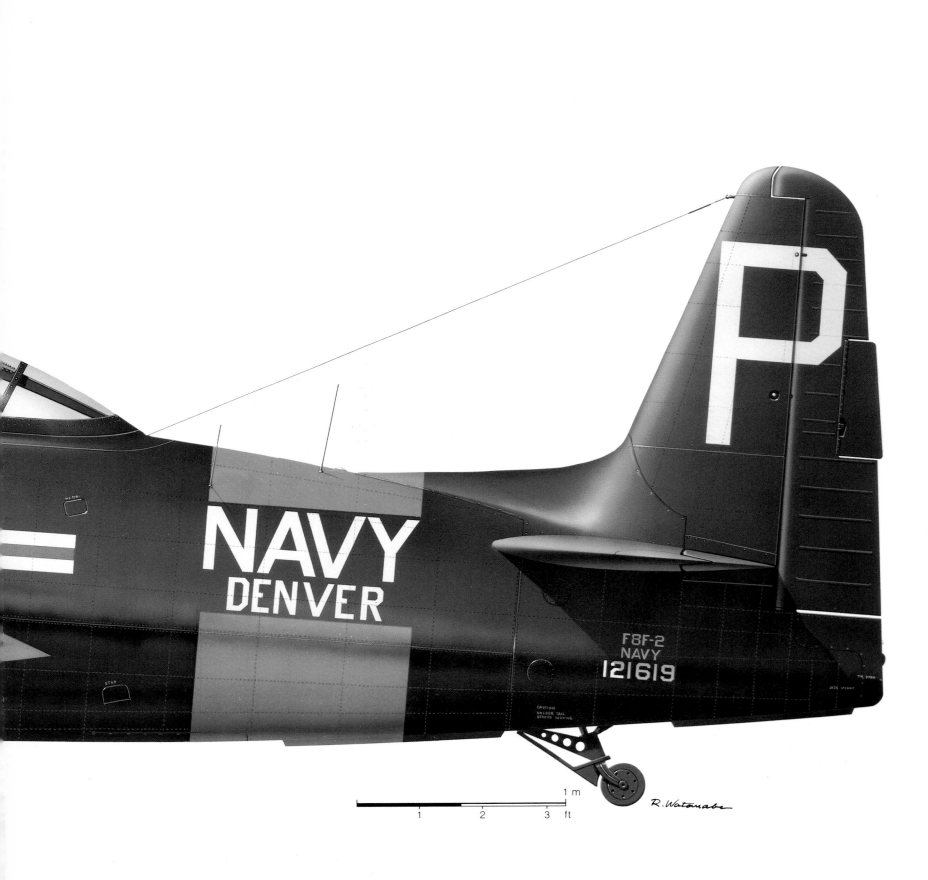

R. Watanabe

minimum takeoff, maximum climb, and heavy armament; range was a secondary consideration. It just missed the war in the Pacific; it was scheduled for operational deployment with the Fleet during the summer of 1945. The F8F-2 model was built in 1948 and 1949, and differed from the F8F-1 models in the taller vertical tail assembly, a re-

vised cowling, and the installation of four 20-mm. cannon instead of .50-cal. machineguns. A modified F8F-2 set a new world speed record of 483. 041 mph. for piston-engined planes in August, 1969. This Bearcat is pictured as it looked around 1950 when flown by pilots of a Naval Reserve unit at Denver, Colorado.

The Great Marianas Turkey Shoot

The largest naval air battle of all time took place off the Mariana Islands in the Philippine Sea on 19 June, 1944. When it was over, Japan's naval air strength was devastated. Only 35 aircraft were left operational in Admiral Ozawa's First Mobile Fleet.

The fight was in the hands of the Hellcat pilots from the very beginning. Their average kill ratio during combat was better than ten to one. But there was a final twist to the battle; a late night recovery, after the longest mission flown by Naval aircraft during the war, cost the U.S. Navy 80 aircraft and 38 aircrew.

battle. The air arm was embarked on nine carriers, and totalled 430 aircraft, of which about one-third were Zero fighters. The supporting force consisted of 13 cruisers, with an air component of 43 floatplanes for scouting and observation, and 28 destroyer escorts. Additional air power was to be drawn from the First Air Fleet, 540 land-based naval aircraft strung out in detachments along a great arc from Chichijima in the Bonin Islands to the East Indies and the Philippines. To reinforce that air fleet, Japanese planners hoped to be able to fly in aircraft from the home islands and from Southeast Asia.

Ozawa's fleet was based at Tawi-tawi in the southern Philippines, where they were near the oil resources of Borneo. From there, they could strike anywhere in the Philippine Sea. The Japanese battle strategy was to wait for

Fighting Fifteen Cdr. Dave McCampbell in the lead, prepares for launch from the *Essex* (CV-9). The white bar is the unofficial recognition marking; later, *Essex* aircraft would sport a geometric 'butterfly' made of white triangles. (National Archives)

This is the story of that great battle which officially is known as the Battle of the Philippine Sea, but best known as the "Great Marianas Turkey Shoot".

The Japanese were ready to make a major naval offensive in the Pacific by mid-1944. After some earlier indecisive battles and some reverses, they had built their warship and aircraft strength to substantial numbers. The First Mobile Fleet, under Vice Admiral Jisaburo Ozawa, centred on the Imperial Navy's first-line strength. Five battleships, including the massive *Yamato* and the *Musashi*, headed the order of

the next American amphibious assault to form. Then Ozawa's force would sail to intercept it and force the battle. His aircraft, plus the half-thousand from the First Air Fleet, would ravage the U.S. naval air strength while his bombers and torpedo planes attacked and destroyed the surface vessels.

The Japanese aircraft had a range advantage; everyone, from fighters to bombers, could out-cruise anything the U.S. Navy had in the air. That range offered a tactical advantage to Ozawa; he would attempt to use it, and

Bataan-based F6F-5s, their rudders carrying the letter T for identification, fly above Japanese waters, 21 June, 1945. (National Archives)

to supplement it by landing his carrier-based aircraft at shore bases so that they could be rearmed and refuelled to return to the fight. That shuttle technique and the basic striking range of about 800 miles (1300 km) that the First Mobile Fleet used in planning its air battles, were expected to give Ozawa the edge over his adversaries.

He needed some kind of an advantage, because on a one-for-one basis, he was inferior. He was up against Task Force 58, already a Navy legend, and then a tough, disciplined, skilled and driven fighting combine. TF 58 had seven large fast carriers and eight light fast carriers, with a total complement of 891 aircraft. They were the foundation of the fleet's strength; but just in case a gunnery battle developed, Vice Admiral Marc Mitscher had seven heavy battleships in the task force. There were additional warships: 21 cruisers with 65 floatplanes and 69 destroyers. The amphibious force they were supporting and defending included its own carriers, seven escort types with a total of 169 embarked aircraft. Mitscher also had available some long-range aircraft, Consolidated PB4Ys out of Admiralty Island, and PBYs operating from Saipan.

The two air fleets were about equal in numbers: 1,013 Japanese planes of all types against 1,125 American aircraft. In all classes of ships, Ozawa was outnumbered and outgunned. An unseen and unknown number of submarines could become part of the action on either side.

Mitscher's airmen had been in the Marianas since about 11 June, seizing and holding air superiority there as the amphibious forces landed and secured the ground. Japan's naval strategists decided that it was now, or perhaps never, and ordered Ozawa to sea. The First Mobile Fleet sailed from its anchorage at Tawi-tawi on June 13. They were tailed by U.S. submarines as they entered the Philippine Sea through the San Bernardino straits.

The U.S. fleet, now aware that Ozawa was on the move, sailed out to meet him and concentrated west of Tinian Island, about 180 miles at sea. Both sides had scouting planes aloft, flying search patterns they hoped would reveal the enemy's fleet. The Japanese scored the first success; they spotted Task Force 58 and were not seen by the Americans.

Ozawa launched the first element of his air strike at 0830 on 19 June, and, in a little more than a half-hour, was in trouble. The U.S.S. *Albacore*, one of the subs that had been at Ozawa's heels, fired a torpedo spread that hit the Japanese flagship carrier *Taiho*. Between the first launch and 1130, Ozawa's carriers sent off three more waves of attackers. It took them three hours to get their 326 planes airborne.

Soon after the last wave had left, the *Shokaku* was torpedoed by the U.S.S. *Cavalla*. Hit by three tin fish at 1220, *Shokaku* fell behind the main force, burning.

Mitscher had split his Task Force 58 into five Task Groups that included four separate carrier components. They took up a loose, widespread formation and steamed into the easterly trade winds. Their Hellcats began the continuous cycle of combat air patrol launches, orbits and recoveries.

At three minutes after ten, the battleship *Alabama* picked up the first radar returns from the oncoming Japanese. Lt. Joe Eggert, Fighter Director Officer, saw what was about to happen and scrambled Hellcats from five carriers: *Cowpens*, *Essex*, *Hornet*, *Monterey*, and *Princeton*. Within minutes they were climbing to 25,000 feet (7600 m) under full military power. The Hellcats coming back from a strike on Guam were held in orbit west of the fleet to intercept any torpedo bombers in the attacking force.

Then the Japanese did an incredible thing. They orbited for about 15 minutes, miles away from the target area, while their leaders gave very detailed briefings on the attack to the flight elements. On board the *Lexington*, Lt. Charles A. Sims intercepted the transmissions, which were broadcast in the clear, and translated them for Eggert's benefit.

All of Mitscher's carriers had turned southeast for the scramble takeoff of every available Hellcat. There were 82 already airborne, either on CAP or returning from Guam, and the carriers fired another 140 into the blue in about 15 minutes. All the bomber and torpedo aircraft were launched also, to clear the carrier decks for continuous Hellcat CAP operations.

First visual contact was made by Cdr. Charles W. Brewer, leading two sections of Hellcats from VF-15. He spotted the Japanese, who were about 50 miles (80 km) from the fleet and at 18,000 feet (5500 m) At 1035 Brewer keyed his mike: "Tallyho! Twenty-four rats (bombers), 16 hawks (fighters) and no fish (torpedo planes)!" He missed seeing another 16 fighters that were high above and well behind the first attacking wave.

Brewer half-rolled, pulled through and dived into the Japanese fighter escort, his seven wingmates close behind. He destroyed four Zeros in the first few minutes of a fierce combat that broke and dispersed the raiders with heavy losses. The second wave was sighted at 1107, seen by radar in the same incredible briefing orbit. Once again, the *Essex* Hellcats were first on the scene, led by Air Group Commander McCampbell. They hammered the Japanese hard; McCampbell himself got five torpedo bombers. The second wave of attackers suffered heavy losses and, like the first, was driven from the target area after an ineffective assault.

There was a two-hour midday lull, another tactical error by the Japanese, and then their third force arrived at 1320. Some had become lost on the way, and so only about 20 aircraft tried to attack. They were beaten off, losing seven in the uneven combat.

The fourth strike was vectored in error by the Japanese controllers to a stretch of open sea without a target in sight. They split into three separate groups with the hope of finding their targets. One group, carrier-based, turned for home, but others continued on. One formation sighted and attacked a Navy task group, but did little damage. The other formation headed to Orote field on Guam.

The dive-bombers that had been launched to wait out the battle tired of doing nothing, and got permission to

Someone just got that Zeke! (National Archives)

strike Orote airfield. They hit it hard, cratering the runways extensively with their bombs. The Japanese 652nd Air Group, hoping to recover at Orote, made their approach and were jumped in the landing pattern by some fifty Hellcats. The Americans claimed 30 Japanese aircraft.

The Japanese heading back to their carriers were sighted by two TBFs and their single Hellcat escort. The Navy trio swung their aircraft into the attack, and were joined almost immediately by another pair of Avengers and a Hellcat. Among them, they shot down seven Zeros. One TBF was hit in the tail, doing no serious damage.

The day's last fight took place over Orote. Brewer was leading a fighter sweep when his section was bounced by Zeros. He and his wingman were killed on the first pass. Perhaps a dozen Japanese fighters mixed it up with the remaining pair of F6Fs. The fight broke; the two Hellcats escaped. And all the Japanese aircraft were either destroyed or severely damaged in their attempts to land on the potholed airfield.

The Japanese stragglers returned to their remaining carriers, now two fewer. At about 1500, an explosion had ripped the *Shokaku* apart, and she sank. Within minutes, a frightening roar erupted from within the *Taiho* and, mortally wounded, she also sank.

After the engineering officers had made their inspections, Ozawa got the bad news: He had about 100

Colt Browning machine-guns,
12.7 mm (0.5 in) Cartridges,
200 rounds for each gun with
provisions for 400 each.

Air-to-ground rockets, 12.7 mm (5 in)

F6F-5 Cockpit

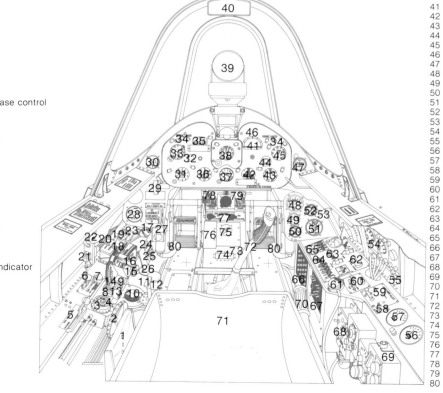

 1 Map case
 2 Elevator trim tab control
 3 Rudder trim tab control
 4 Aileron trim tab control
 5 Tail wheel lock control
 6 Cowl flaps control
 7 Oil cooler shutter control
 8 Fuel tank pressure control
 9 Oil dilution switch
10 Fuel tank selector valve
11 Fuselage droppable tank manual release control
12 Anti-blackout regulator
13 Propeller pitch control
14 Propeller pitch vernier control
15 Engine control quadrant friction knob
16 Mixture control
17 Supercharger control
18 Throttle control
19 Mask microphone switch
20 Wing flaps electric control switch
21 Droppable fuel tank release switch
22 Cockpit light
23 Water injection control switch
24 Auxiliary electric fuel pump switch
25 Intercooler shutter control
26 Fuel tank pipe
27 Landing gear control
28 Landing gear and wing flap position indicator
29 Carburetor protected air control
30 Ignition switch
31 Altimeter
32 Instrument panel light
33 Clock
34 Spare lamps
35 Directional gyro
36 Airspeed indicator
37 Rate of climb indicator
38 Compass
39 Electric gunsight
40 Rear-view mirror

41 Gyro horizon
42 Turn and bank indicator
43 Manifold pressure gauge
44 Gyro horizon caging knob
45 Tachometer
46 Raflector panel
47 Water quantity gauge—A.D.I. system
48 Cylinder head temperature gauge
49 Oil-in temperature gauge
50 Fuel pressure gauge
51 Fuel quantity gauge
52 Oil pressure gauge
53 Cabin sliding hood control
54 Radio controls
55 Cockpit light
56 Landing gear emergency dump pressure gauge
57 Hydraulic system pressure gauge
58 IFF destructor switch
59 Hydraulic pump selector valve
60 Recognition light switch
61 Hand microphone
62 Main electrical distribution panel
63 Generator warning light
64 Radio master control switch
65 Starter switch
66 Manual reset circuit breaker panel
67 Armament panel
68 Radio channel selector
69 IFF controls
70 Hydraulic hand pump
71 Pilot's seat
72 Control column
73 Fresh air duct control
74 Fresh air duct
75 MK-I rocket selector
76 Check-off card
77 Gun charging control
78 Landing gear emergency lowering control
79 Wing folding safety lock control
80 Rudder pedals

Five-inch HVAR rockets being racked on the underwing of one of the *Enterprise*'s Hellcats.
(National Archives)

Ammunition (.50-cal. rounds) being loaded in the ammunition bay of folded Hellcat wing.
(National Archives)

airworthy aircraft left. The Japanese had lost 315, including those knocked out of the skies over Guam, and 22 that went down with the two carriers.

U.S. losses were light; 16 Hellcats were downed, and some ships had been hit, despite the protective screen that the fighters put up over the fleet. But no ships were damaged seriously, and none had been sunk.

Another day was coming, and both sides planned to strike again. They manoeuvered without encountering each other, and the searches flown by both sides turned up no results. Finally, late in the day, Navy planes sighted Ozawa's fleet. It was out near the end of the effective cruising radius of American fighters and bombers, and to launch an attack then meant that the Navy aircraft would be operating at extreme range. The two fleets were about 275 miles (440 km) apart, and Mitscher decided to risk the launch, even though he knew that his aircraft would be returning after dark.

The first Hellcat was fired off the *Lexington* at 1624; 12 minutes later, the last of 236 aircraft, an SBD from the *Lexington*, lifted off her deck.

They found the Japanese, in a formation of three carrier groups and one oiler group, and charged into battle. The Japanese, over home territory, had the advantage; they launched about 75 Zeros. Those fighters and the anti-aircraft shot down 12 U.S. planes. But it was a very uneven trade; the Japanese lost the carrier *Hiyo* to a torpedo attack. Other ships were hit and damaged, and about 30 Japanese aircraft planes were shot down.

By 1935, all the U.S. Navy aircraft were headed homeward, leaving behind three Japanese ships sunk and seven damaged. Their toughest times lay ahead; they were coming home long after dark.

Mitscher, who had been sweating out the return of his pilots, passed a curt order to turn on the lights of the ships. It was unheard of in wartime; the fleet always travelled in a complete blackout at night. But this time, Marc Mitscher had

his pilots out there in the dark, and he wanted to give them the best possible chance to get home safely.

It may be a little harsh to call what followed a panic. But the recovery of so many aircraft, all of them low on fuel and manned by pilots relatively inexperienced in night operations, was just that. The order was to land on any carrier, and they did. Aircraft shot the approach in formation, with pilots jockeying for position. Planes landed on top of planes. Others landed alongside the carriers or the covering destroyers in the water, out of fuel. Machines landed in tandem on carrier decks, one picking up the aft wires and one picking up the forward, or worse, missing them and crashing into the barrier or other aircraft.

The losses were heavy. The two days of fighting with the Japanese in the greatest naval air battle of all time had cost the U.S. Navy 49 planes. But that night landing cost 80 aircraft and 38 aircrew.

But the results still favoured the American force. The Japanese fleet was withdrawing at speed to the temporary shelter of Okinawa. It had lost three heavy carriers, and two more were heavily damaged, out of action for the rest of the war. Only 35 operational aircraft were left to Ozawa. And in contrast, the U.S. Navy had lost no ships at all, all were operational, and they had more than 700 aircraft still embarked.

The U.S. Navy was in undisputed possession of the Philippine Sea, and of the sky above it. The Navy had won one of the decisive battles of World War II, had protected the landings on Saipan, had driven the Japanese out of the arena and had inflicted such losses on them that there was no possible recovery.

Ozawa had lost three-quarters of his airmen, and it was not only the first team that he had lost. It was the only team he had. There were no reserves, and there was no full pipeline of pilots from training schools. It was the end of Japan's carrier air effort.

Cat's Eyes at Midnight

The F6F-5N's cockpit radar display. (David A. Anderton)

Night raids by both Pacific antagonists were, if not routine, at least not uncommon. Given a moonlit night, and some recognizable landmarks defined by reflections from water, it was within the capabilities of the more-experienced pilots to handle a night mission.

But intercepting and attacking a night mission was a problem of another order of magnitude. Visually, it had to be largely a matter of luck. Perceptions are deceptive in the environment of night flying, and unless a keen-eyed pilot could spot the pale blue exhaust flames from an enemy plane's engines, he stood little chance of completing the intercept.   Radar held the promise of solving that problem. Before the United States had been drawn into the conflict of World War II, the Navy developed a requirement for an airborne intercept (AI) radar with a three-centimeter wavelength. Its primary envisioned use was for night intercepts; its secondary was for attacking surface vessels. The Radiation Laboratory at the Massachusetts Institute of Technology was assigned the job in January, 1941, and straight-away scientists began component development on a prototype set, the AI-3 (AN/SCR-537). Design of the specific system for the Navy began in August. In December, because the Radiation Laboratory was a prototype shop only, the Navy awarded a production contract to the Sperry Gyroscope Co. for a set designated the AIA. By late 1942, Sperry had the unit in full production for Hellcat deliveries.

The company delivered 604 sets of the equipment for installation in F6F-3E and – 3N aircraft. By late 1943, the AIA designation had been changed to AN/APS-4 (APS = Airborne Pulse Search). It was mounted in a pod on the Hellcat's right wing, in an unsightly protuberance that caused all manner of comment and not a little apprehension on the part of pilots who wondered what that thing would do to the drag, and particularly to the stall, characteristics of the Hellcat. (It slowed the aircraft by about 20 mph (32 km/h), and it triggered a right-wing drop in a stall.)

A proficient operator of the APS-4 could pick up a target at a maximum distance of about four miles (six kilometers). As a first attempt, the equipment was not too bad, but there was room for improvement, and Westinghouse Electric Corp. got a Navy contract for a follow-on set designated the APS-6. It turned out, as all developments of a basic unit seem to, considerably heavier. It was still installed in the same pod on the right wing. But the reliable range was about five miles in the search mode, and it would work down to a minimum range of about 120 yards (110 m). Ideal firing range during night interceptions was about 250 yards (230 m). The APS-6 weighed 242 pounds (110 kilograms), and it cost $10,936 for each unit. Westinghouse produced 2,161 of them by the end of the war, and they were installed on both the Hellcat and the Corsair night fighter versions.

Four sub-models of the Hellcat carried the new electronic gear into the air: The F6F-3E, -3N, -5E and -5N. The first of these, the F6F-3E, was equipped with an early form of the airborne search radar designated ASH or ASD-1. Only 18 aircraft were so equipped and may never have reached the fleet as operational planes.

The real developmental night fighter was the F6F-3N, carrying the new AIA radar into battle. It was a basic -3 Hellcat with some special equipment and modifications to fit it for the night-fighter mission. In addition to the radar, the -3N had a redesigned instrument panel with red lighting to interfere the least with the pilot's night vision. The panel mounted a radar altimeter (AN/APN-1) and the relatively new IFF (Identification Friend or Foe) equipment (AN/APX-2). The standard Hellcat windshield was curved plexiglass in front, backed by a protective slab of bullet-proof glass. The combination caused internal reflections in the cockpit, and so it was replaced by a single flat panel on production F6F-3N Hellcats and all subsequent models.

First deliveries of the AIA equipment began with the receipt of six sets in September, 1943, by which time Grumman had delivered 19 of the aircraft supposed to carry those radars.

The final version of the night-fighting Hellcat, the F6F-5N, differed only in the type of radar installed. Deliveries of the APS-6 unit began in February, 1944, and continued at a rate that considerably exceeded the Navy's acceptances of the fighters. It was probably just as well; early radar sets were noted for their unreliability and, in the pressure of wartime, a malfunctioning set was likely to be yanked out entirely and replaced by a completely new unit. Lots of spares were necessary, and perhaps that explains why the production rate of APS-6 sets was about three times the rate of F6F-5N production.

According to a Navy Aviation Planning Directive 85-A-44 of 26 September, 1944, night-fighter Hellcats were to be assigned to carrier air day-fighter groups as well as to the dedicated night-fighter groups formed and attached to both heavy and light carriers. In a standard carrier air group aboard one of the fast carriers, there were to be four -5N and two -5E Hellcats. Each dedicated night-fighter group attached to a heavy carrier was to be equipped with the -5E and -5N in equal numbers. On the light carriers, only the -5N fighters were to be assigned.

The same directive showed that the Navy envisaged a final total of 54 Hellcat squadrons assigned to the heavy carriers. Of these, 46 would be fighter squadrons for daytime operations. Four would be -5N squadrons, and two would be -5E squadrons; all six would be dedicated night-fighter units. There would be 16 squadrons each of the -5E and -5N models, equipping the planned 32 night-fighter squadrons to be assigned to carrier air groups that would be dedicated only to night fighting. And 16 squadrons of -5N models were to be assigned for dedicated night fighting air groups on board the light carriers.

As finally put into service, the night-fighter Hellcats served with considerably fewer squadrons than the grand plan had foretold. Eight Navy Squadrons and five Marine squadrons were the only night-fighter units to see combat during the war. The Navy's night fighters worked as a team, using the powerful shipboard search radars and fighter directors as the primary source of attack information. The position of the bogie, detected on the radars, was relayed to the airborne "Bat" team, generally a single radar-equipped TBF accompanied by a pair of night-fighter Hellcats. Steering vectors guided the team to the general vicinity of the enemy, and at that point, the radar of the TBF was used to direct the fighters on the closing intercept. Their own radars would be brought into use then, and would supply the primary information to make the intercept and attack the enemy. But the final judgment was made by the old-fashioned human eyeball. After the radar indicated that the fighter had closed to firing range, the pilot almost invariably turned his vision from the scope presentation to look forward through the windshield, and would complete the attack visually.

Hardly two months after the first APS-4 sets had been delivered, the first attempts at night interception were made by U.S. Navy pilots in the campaign in the Gilbert Islands. They resulted in both triumph and tragedy. And, as is so often the case, the price paid was far too high for the results achieved.

Task Group 50.2 was lying off Makin Island in the Gilberts. The fast carrier *Enterprise*, keystone of the force, had been on the receiving end of night attacks by a few Japanese "Betty" (Mitsubishi G4M) bombers. For two nights, the bombers attacked, unmolested. Then, on 24 November, a "Bat" team from Fighting Two, led by Lt. Cdr. Edward H. O'Hare, tried an intercept which failed. "Butch" O'Hare had become intensely interested in night fighting; as commander of Air Group Six, he was responsible for the defence of the *Enterprise*. Any means that would improve his chances of staving off a Japanese attack interested him.

Two nights later, the bombers came back in a force of about 30. A "Bat" team was aloft, and the TBF picked up the telltale returns of the bomber formation on the radar scope. The Hellcats were vectored into the area, but found nothing. O'Hare, flying an F6F-3N, and his teammate, flying a standard day model, stayed in the area and waited. Soon after, the radar on board *Enterprise* picked up the Japanese, and gave the Hellcats a course to bring them nearer to the formation. The three planes, flying a fairly tight formation for night-time operations, closed on the bombers. The pilot of

the TBF found the target on his scope was within effective gunnery range. He fired the forward machine-gun, a single synchronized .50-cal on the starboard cowling, and then pulled up and to the left to give his turret gunner a chance to use the twin fifties back in that position. The inflammable "Betty" staggered, caught fire, and plunged to the dark water below. In the manoeuvring, the formation had opened up and O'Hare was, he believed, too far away from the Avenger. The Fighter Director below, still working the radar screen, called a second set of bogies, and immediately after, the TBF pilot sighted a pair of bombers. O'Hare asked him to turn on his recognition lights so that the fighters could form on him, but the Avenger pilot understandably refused, not wanting to give the Japanese a chance to spot him in the night sky. He did, however, flash his lights once or twice, and then proceeded to shoot down a second "Betty" with his forward gun while his turret gunner fired at a third.

Once again under control of the Fighter Director, the TBF began an orbit and turned on its recognition lights. The Hellcats switched on theirs and began to move in close to the torpedo bomber. As O'Hare closed in from astern, the TBF turret gunner fired at what he believed was an unidentified plane crossing the formation from behind. It was, probably, O'Hare's Hellcat that he hit, and it was the last combat for the Medal of Honour winner. Two Japanese bombers had been downed in this first successful night interception and attack by the radar-equipped "Bat" team. But the loss of O'Hare was not an even trade.

During the Marshall Islands campaign, detachments of night-fighter squadrons were assigned to five carriers, and occasionally they were sent out against the Japanese. But the trouble of night launches and recoveries after a day full of hard work for the deck crew didn't seem worth it, and the night 'cats were seldom sent out as a result.

That was in early 1944. By late in the year, the situation had been changed by the formation of dedicated night-fighter squadrons attached to a specified carrier for after-dark operations only. The *Independence* was the first carrier so designated. She carried a complement of 14 F6F-5Ns manned by the pilots of VF(N)-41, plus eight TBM-1Ds equipped with search radar. Five standard day-fighter F6F-5s were also assigned, to fly combat air patrols during the daylight hours.

Typical of their action was the job they did on the night of 12 October. The Japanese routinely sent out long-range bombers to act as fleet shadowers; they spotted the positions of the ships, reported activities, and occasionally pressed home a bombing attack. That night, the "Bat" teams of VF(N)-41 were airborne when they were directed to a group of Mitsubishi G4Ms that were up to the usual trick. One after another, the Hellcats approached, fired, and shot down five "Betty" bombers.

Marine NF squadrons were active with the radar-equipped Hellcats, and racked up an impressive total score before the war was over. But the most remembered association of the Marine units with night-fighting requirements was summed up tersely in the war diary of Marine Night Fighting Squadron 541 (VMF(N)-541) for December, 1944:

A formation of F6F-5Ns. (National Archives)

"The Commanding General, Far East Air Forces, requested that the F6F night fighters replace the (Army Air Forces) P-61 night fighters at Tacloban Drome (on Leyte, in the Philippines) for several weeks. The P-61 had not sufficient range or speed to perform the necessary duties required by the 308th Bomb Wing."

In December, 1944, and January, 1945, the Marine VMF(N)-541 Hellcats shot down 22 aircraft at night. Their efforts were not unrewarded; the squadron received an Army Distinguished Unit Citation, the only Marine Corps aviation unit to be so recognized.

Marine unit night victories totalled 106, most of them scored in Hellcats. "Black Mac's Killers," the informal name for VMF(N)-533, was the highest scorer, with 35 Japanese to its credit. VMF(N)-542, based at Yontan field, Okinawa, began its night-fighting career late in the war. From 16 April, 1945, to V-J Day, they accounted for 17 Japanese aircraft and lost only two of their own.

In the closing months of the war, studies and tests were still being conducted to improve the quality and effectiveness of night fighting. One such series was a tactical evalu-

ation of searchlights flown at NAS Patuxent River, Maryland. Two Hellcats – one a -3N model and the other a -5N – were fitted with two different types of searchlights and sent up to intercept a variety of aircraft of different size and performance, varying from other F6Fs to a USAAF Consolidated B-24 bomber.

The planned tactic was to use the radar for finding the target, and for closing for the attack. The searchlight would then be turned on for the attack itself. No matter that the British had tried the same idea earlier in the war and had abandoned it in favour of concentrating on radar. The programme ran from 3 March, 1945, until June 11, and required 36 hours of flight tests. The conclusion: The disadvantages outweighed the advantages and, besides, airborne intercept radar was coming along nicely by then.

There were Navy and Marine night-fighter aces, although for apparent reasons their scores were less than the top tallies achieved by such pilots as McCampbell and Vraciu. But their contribution was a major one to the development of radar for interception and attack.

The Lingering Death of an Empire

Hellcat 24, from the *Bunker Hill*, over Subic Bay, Manila.

Japan's carrier force had been decisively beaten in the battle of the Philippine Sea, and Saipan had been lost. The irreplaceable pilots that perished in the "Great Marianas Turkey Shoot," and the further decimation that had resulted from continuing combat losses, left few aviators of any competence and fewer with any knowledge and experience to lead. Attacks on Japanese merchant shipping, particularly tankers, had reduced drastically the flow of supplies to the home islands. The Japanese Navy was so low on fuel that it could not have the freedom it once enjoyed. Instead of putting to sea, it stayed in port, scraping together enough reserves for an occasional foray.

It must have been painfully apparent to any Japanese who thought about the situation that the country was doomed to lose the war. But those were different times, and there were different customs. It has never been easy for people with totally different cultural heritages to understand each other. And so, from here and now, it may seem strange that the Japanese continued to resist, and to do so desperately and bravely, even suicidally. There and then, however, that was the situation.

It must be said that the Japanese did not seem very adept at learning from bitter experience. They never mastered the strategies, tactics or techniques of sustained carrier air war. A few brilliant strikes were overshadowed by a long succession of unimaginative campaigns and battles fought poorly. In aircraft design, they did not realize, until too late, that air war was not entirely a matter of individual combat, pilot against pilot, in a mad melee of manoeuvring. Air war was a matter of striking fast first, and getting out to strike again. The important design requirements were firepower, armour, and self-sealing tanks. Low wing loading, and the ability to perform astounding aerobatics, had gone out in the '30s with the death of the biplane.

It's an old story now, but the Hellcat was inferior to the Japanese fighters in many respects. If the contest had been to see who could turn tighter, loop faster, roll more quickly, zoom vertically, or split-S in a split second, the Zeros would have won, hands down. But it wasn't that kind of a contest, and the Hellcat was designed for a different kind of air combat. And in that role, doing that job, it was infinitely superior to anything the Japanese aircraft industry ever thought of producing.

And the Americans continued to learn from combat experience, and to apply the lessons to the design of their aircraft and other weapons – in most cases. True, they stayed with an atrocious torpedo, an absolutely appalling performer that accounted for many Americans lost in attacks. The U.S. Navy also never fully appreciated the importance of really long-range scouting and search planes; the Japanese had it all over them in that regard. But when it came to finding out what a Hellcat could do, and using it in the best way possible, the Americans had no peers.

And so the F6F became a fighter-bomber. It would haul bombs further, and drop them more accurately, than the "Beast", the Helldiver that had been designed specifically to do that very job. (In fairness, it must be said that late models of the Curtiss aircraft resolved many of the difficulties of the earlier models, but they were too late to have any real effect on the Pacific war.)

Carrier air groups cannot afford to be tied to a single concept of employment for their aircraft. Portable air power demands a versatile, flexible and dynamic force structure, using aircraft that themselves are versatile and flexible. During the war, the basic structure of the carrier air groups, and the uses of their aircraft, changed to reflect the changing demands of the campaigns.

For most of the war described to this point, the standard makeup of a carrier air group was 36 fighters, 36 bombers, and 18 torpedo planes. In August, 1944, that was changed to a mix of 54 fighters, 24 bombers and 18 torpedo planes. Further, those 54 fighters were to include four night fighters and two photographic conversions of the standard fighters.

The U.S. Navy continued to roll westward, striking in the Western Carolines in late July, 1944, supporting the occupation of Palau and Morotai in September, and then heading for the Philippines and the invasion and occupation of Leyte.

And there, the Japanese introduced a new weapon of air war with frightening potential. It inflicted more punishment on the U.S. Navy than that service had ever felt before. And, for a while, it appeared to be unstoppable.

That weapon was, of course, the suicide attack by individual Japanese pilots who deliberately guided their aircraft to crash on Navy ships. On 25 October, off Leyte, the first of these planned attacks hit and sank the escort carrier

St. Lo CVE-63. In later action, a dozen more carriers of all three classes were hit and damaged, some severely, by kamikazes from Japanese bases in the Philippines.

As one countermeasure, the Navy increased the complement of fighters on board their iron carriers. From late November, a carrier air group on board one of the large fast carriers was to have 73 fighters, and only 15 each of bombers and torpedo planes. The fighters were formed into two squadrons of 36 each, with one more Hellcat for the Air Group Commander himself, and they included four F6F-5N, two F6F-5P, and two F6F-5E aircraft.

The damage done by the Japanese kamikazes in the battle of Leyte Gulf was only part of the toll. The light carrier *Princeton*, with its "cat-mouth" Hellcats of VF-27 embarked, was bombed. She burned, and later exploded, killing many of a rescue force from the cruiser *Birmingham* that had pulled alongside to assist.

In December, the fleet supported the landings on Mindoro Island in the Philippines. Task Force 38 under Vice Admiral John S. McCain, sent its seven heavy and eight light carriers to launch fighter sweeps over the island on 14 December, holding down the Japanese air elements and assuring air supremacy over the battleground. McCain's pilots flew a continuous cycle of combat air patrol over the fleet and over the landing areas, relieving the Hellcats on station in the air. Fighters were always airborne and ready for any Japanese aircraft that came by. If any did, it was quickly

hammered out of the sky by the "Big Blue Blanket". The Japanese lost 341 aircraft in that campaign, and the major share of that loss was credited to the carrier-based Hellcats of TF38. In early January, it was the turn of Luzon Island. Again, the kamikazes hurtled past the protective fighter screens, through the thick anti-aircraft fire, and slammed into the decks or hulls of carrier after carrier. The escort carrier *Ommaney Bay* was sunk, and her sister-ships *Manila Bay* and the *Savo Island*, were damaged in early attacks. Later, it was the turn of two more *Bay* class escorts, the *Kadashan Bay* and the *Kitkun Bay*, as well as the *Salamaua*.

Those attacks on the carriers really harrassed the Navy. The escorts, lightly built and nicknamed "Kaiser coffins" after the shipyards that developed their construction techniques, were singled out by the Japanese as targets. It is surprising, in the light of the vulnerability of those small carriers, that more were not fatally stricken when the kamikazes hit. But superb damage-control work and fire-fighting by their crews saved most of the carriers from severe destruction and probable sinking.

McCain's TF38 was subdivided into four battle groups. Seven heavy carriers and four light carriers were apportioned among three of the groups. The fourth – a dedicated night operations battle group – deployed a single heavy carrier and a single light carrier. Their pilots concentrated on hitting enemy aircraft, in the air when they were there, but mostly on the ground, where they were kept by the incessant

Fighting Twenty-Seven's "Cat-Mouth" Hellcats

(National Archives)

Nose art was conspicuous by its absence from the side cowling panels of the average Hellcat. There were a few land-based Marine F6Fs that are known to have carried some decorations, but all fleet Hellcats were marked only with numbers, the standard insignia, and carrier identifiers.

All, that is, except for the Hellcats of VF-27, aboard the *Princeton*. Three VF-27 pilots – Carl Brown, Richard Stambook, and Robert Burnell – conceived the idea of marking their Hellcats with a distinctive "cat-mouth" design, borrowing the concept from the many "shark-mouth" noses that have been used through the years on fighters. Burnell personally hand-painted most of the designs on the planes.

The *Princeton* was attached to Task Group 38.3, under Rear Admiral Forrest C. Sherman. On 24 October, 1944, the force was off the coast of eastern Luzon in the Philippines, about 150 miles (240 km) out of Manila. They were seen by a Japanese observation plane, which radioed a warning to its main force. The Japanese launched an attack, using land-based bombers from Luzon, and carrier-based aircraft from Admiral Ozawa's fleet. They arrived over the Task Group in the early morning, and *Princeton* Hellcats were flying combat air patrol when they spotted the Japanese.

It was an uneven battle. VF-27 had only eight of its F6F-5s aloft, a standard number for the job, and they roared into the fight at odds of ten to one. "We held off 80 planes for about 15 minutes," Lt. Carl Brown said later. "We had to get them before they got our ships . . . It had been drilled into us that the primary task of a Navy fighter pilot is to protect his ship."

But heroics on that scale couldn't save the *Princeton*; she was hit by a single bomb at 0938. Normally a single bomb does limited damage and causes casualties; but this single missile hit the aft elevator. Six Avengers, fully gassed and loaded with weapons for a strike, blew up almost simultaneously. The *Princeton* crew fought the fires, but it was a hopeless task. In mid-afternoon, a thunderous blast rocked the ship. Her stern was blown off, and the explosion, the fireball, the concussion, and flying debris caused hideous and high casualties.

With the carrier in flames and her deck unable to receive aircraft, the Hellcats of VF-27 had to land on other carriers. And there they ran afoul of the Navy's official views on nose art. No matter that they had just lost their ship, in spite of extreme efforts to save her. No matter that the fighter pilots of VF-27 had developed an esprit-de-corps built around those "cat-mouth" designs The decorations had to go; they were not Navy.

And so they were removed; with a few days all the VF-27 Hellcats looked like any other Hellcats in the fleet.

But some photographs remain, and from them, the artist has re-created a typical Hellcat of VF-27 as it looked on the day the *Princeton* was lost. It's a tribute to VF-27, and to all naval fighter pilots whose first thoughts were of the defence of their ships.

pressure of the Hellcats' combat air patrol. When Luzon was declared secure by the commanders of the ground force, McCain took TF38 into the South China Sea and spent a few days there sinking Japanese shipping with well-timed air strikes. At the end of the fight for Luzon and the excursion into the South China Sea, McCain's men reckoned they had destroyed about 700 Japanese aircraft and had sunk about 365,000 tons of shipping.

Once again the force structure changed. In early January, the Navy began the commissioning of 18 new VBF (Heavier-than-Air Bomber Fighter) squadrons within the existing carrier air groups. The reason was that the Japanese were no longer believed capable of mounting a serious air threat. More bombers would be needed for the coming planned invasion of Japan and the prerequisite air interdiction that would be orchestrated with strategic bombing by the B-29 force. One of the necessary tasks to be accomplished before the B-29s could operate effectively from the Marianas bases was the capture of Iwo Jima. Garrisoned by the Japanese, and base for an air element that included bombers and fighters, Iwo was about halfway between the Marianas and Japan. It was to become a valuable emergency landing area for troubled B-29s, and would justify the bloody losses that were suffered in taking it.

Task Force 58, under Mitscher, was deployed on a covering operation to hit Tokyo on 16 and 17 February, with the Iwo Jima invasion scheduled for 19 February. They struck that city again on 25 February, bombing and shelling air and naval installations and ships. Following those strikes, Mitscher's pilots claimed the destruction of 648 aircraft and 30,000 tons of shipping.

And off Iwo, the kamikazes struck again, sinking the escort carrier *Bismarck Sea*. Their attacks hit and severely damaged the *Saratoga*, and did minor hurt to the *Lunga Point*.

Iwo Jima was declared secure 16 March, although B-29 crews making emergency landings there a few days later were still reporting Japanese small-arms fire as they approached the field. Two days later, Mitscher's Task Force 58 joined the campaign against Okinawa, a fortress island. His first task was to strike Japanese installations on Kyushu Island, the departure point for reinforcements on the way to

A Zero (A6M5a) diving on the *USS Essex*.

Okinawa. His ten heavy carriers and six light carriers launched their aircraft against the Japanese home island in a series of devastating strikes. They destroyed 482 planes by air attack, most of them on the ground, and an additional 46 were pulverized by naval gunfire. By March 23, TF58 was back off Okinawa and had begun to send combat sorties over that island.

The kamikaze was the only offensive weapon left to Japan. Her carrier force was destroyed, her airmen lost, her navy reduced to a few ships cowering in port, her distant garrisons overwhelmed. The kamikaze effort was potentially a deadly weapon; yet it required more skill than the young and inexperienced pilots had absorbed in their brief training. Like so many of the Japanese tactics, this one also leaves the question "What if . . .?" hanging in the air.

To the best of their abilities, these highly motivated, deeply patriotic, devoted subjects of the Emperor coolly and deliberately dashed themselves and their planes against the unyielding steel hull, the planked deck, or the armoured superstructure of Naval vessels.

In their last action, coded "Kikusui" (Floating Chrysanthemum), Army and Navy pilots together pledged to die in their attacks against the American fleet off Okinawa.

They came in formations, their war-weary aircraft scattered in loose geometries across the skies. Often they were intercepted on the way, and they died in the air instead of the way they had planned.

USS Essex takes a *kamikaze* hit aft of the forward elevator. She was able to survive thanks largely to damage-control improvements.

The *Yamato* off Leyte Gulf.

One such intercept tells the whole story. Lt. Eugene Valencia, on his second combat tour, was up with his "Flying Circus," also known as the "VF-9 Mowing Machine". His three hand-picked wingmen – Lts. James French, Harris Mitchel, and Clinton Smith – orbited with him at 5,000 feet above a picket destroyer. The ship's radar was being interpreted by a Fighter Director Officer on board, and he was reading the bearing and height of an approaching gaggle of Japanese aircraft. He vectored the Hellcats toward them. Valencia's section slashed into the formation and began the one-sided blood letting. Out of 38 planes in the attacking group, the "Mowing Machine" destroyed 14. They claimed nine more as probably destroyed, and six damaged. And there was not a single bullet hole in any of the four Hellcats.

The Navy, after it had time to collect battle reports and apply some objective thought to the raw data, estimated that the Japanese expended as many as 1,500 aircraft in a series of seven kamikaze attacks between 6 April and 28 May. Certainly the Navy had never been so punished.

No carriers were sunk; but 12 were hit and damaged and some of those had to be returned to a naval shipyard for major repairs. The list reads like a roll-call of the carriers on the scene: *Enterprise*, *Intrepid*, *Yorktown*, *Franklin*, *Wasp*, *San Jacinto*, *Hancock*, *Essex*, and *Bunker Hill*, all from TF58; *Wake Island*, *Sangamon* and *Natoma Bay*, all from TF52.

Not only aircraft featured in these suicidal attacks. The Japanese Navy finally sortied on its last attempt to strike the Americans, and it was a mission of deliberate self-destruction. They were to attack the U.S. ships lying off Okinawa and fight to the end. If they exhausted their ammunition while they were still above water, they were instructed to run aground so the crews could join in the defence of Okinawa. Flagship on this last attack was the huge *Yamato*. She was escorted by a light cruiser and a screen of eight destroyers. Bottled in the Inland Sea by effective mining that had been done by the B-29s, the *Yamato* force had only one way out. It sailed through the Bungo strait and was seen by American subs, which were operating almost openly in the Japanese waters.

The Japanese ships were found the next morning by a scout from the *Enterprise*; the pilot radioed his position back and the battle began to take shape. Task Force 58 with three of its fast carrier groups already under way toward the threat, launched 75 bombers and 131 torpedo planes with an escort of 180 fighters.

The Japanese had no air cover; the glossy blue planes drove to their targets and pounded the big battleship hard with bombs and torpedoes. She took five direct bomb hits and ten torpedo strikes, rolled over and sank with 2,500 men. The cruiser and four of the destroyers joined her on the bottom. Only the remaining four destroyers escaped, running to Sasebo at their top speed.

The Americans lost a dozen planes. Once again, capital ships had been sunk by air power, and once again the aircraft proved itself to be the basic unit weapon of naval strength.

Finally the ghastly Okinawa campaign ground to a halt. The island had become a charnel-house. Japanese soldiers and civilians had been cut down by every means known to the technology of war, and by a much older and stranger means: Suicide.

If statistics are meaningful in that context, here are some of the Navy's numbers for that campaign:

Naval aircraft flew more than 40,000 combat sorties. They dropped more than 8,500 tons (18,700,000 pounds) of bombs, fired about 50,000 rockets, and shot off countless rounds of ammunition. The pilots claimed a total of 2,516 enemy aircraft destroyed. Marine squadrons, operating from shore bases, claimed 506 Japanese planes downed or otherwise destroyed, and reported that they had dropped 1,800 tons (3,600,000 pounds) of bombs and fired 15,865 rockets during their close air support missions.

The *Essex*, prototypical ship for an entire class of heavy, fast carriers, once again distinguished herself. She had been in combat for 79 consecutive days, a record untouched by any other U.S. carrier during the war.

Now all that remained was the final assault on Japan itself, an invasion that was expected to be the most costly operation of World War II. The forces began to gather their strength for that final battle.

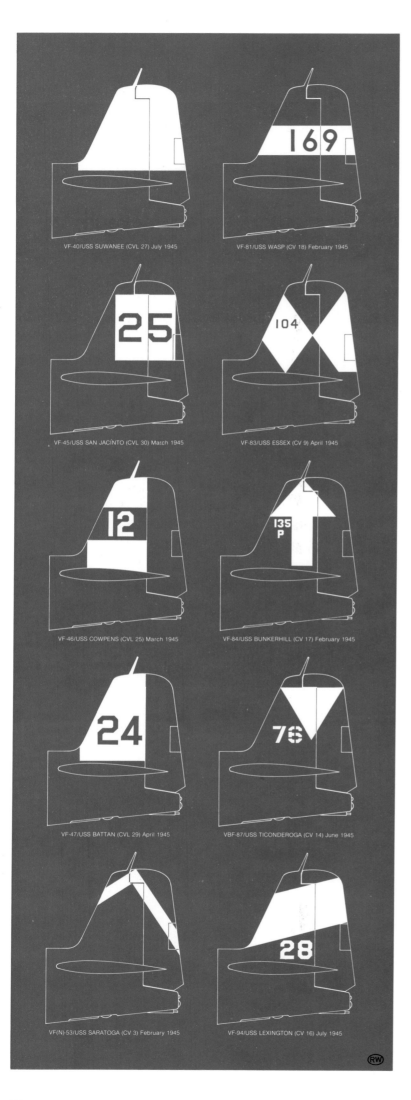

VF-40/USS SUWANEE (CVL 27) July 1945

VF-81/USS WASP (CV 18) February 1945

VF-45/USS SAN JACINTO (CVL 30) March 1945

VF-83/USS ESSEX (CV 9) April 1945

VF-46/USS COWPENS (CVL 25) March 1945

VF-84/USS BUNKERHILL (CV 17) February 1945

VF-47/USS BATTAN (CVL 29) April 1945

VBF-87/USS TICONDEROGA (CV 14) June 1945

VF(N)-53/USS SARATOGA (CV 3) February 1945

VF-94/USS LEXINGTON (CV 16) July 1945

The Last Battle

Early in March, 1945, a cigar-chomping Army Air Forces general made a fateful decision. He ordered his B-29 crews to strip their aircraft of the defensive armament except for tail guns, and to get rid of all unnecessary equipment on board. Then, said Maj. Gen. Curtis E. LeMay, load 'em with incendiaries and bomb the cities from five or six thousand feet (1500 or 1800 metres). The first fire raid, which hit Tokyo, was successful beyond belief, and it was followed by another fire-bombing mission, and another, and another. One by one, the great industrial cities of Japan, the cities built around naval bases, army garrisons and airfields became funeral pyres for thousands.

Much of Japan's dispersed industrial support was destroyed in the raids, burned in the relentless and consuming flames of thermite bombs. Vast numbers of the population had been displaced, were homeless, had lost families, relatives, friends, homes and places to work. And still the Japanese summoned enough reserves of strength and courage to talk of defending their country to the death.

Old men and women trained with bamboo spears. Factory workers slaved to turn out one more aircraft, one more gun, one more shell, knowing that every one would count. Aircraft in every state of repair were prepared for one more flight, and hidden under camouflage or in the ruins of villages and towns, waiting for their last missions. Fuel was collected, barrel by precious barrel, and stored near the concealed aircraft. And all over Japan, the people prepared to face a frightening future.

The U.S. Navy's Third Fleet, commanded by Admiral William F. Halsey, detached Task Force 38 to operate against the Japanese homeland. Vice Admiral McCain, TF38 commander, had 14 available carriers in the strike force, and his operations were supported by a replenishment group and a group dedicated to anti-submarine warfare. Both these support units included escort carriers whose aircraft normally flew CAP, but were also available for supplementing the air strength of the main body of the task force.

The British detached their Carrier Task Force 37 under the Royal Navy's Vice Admiral H. B. Rawlings, and ordered its four carriers and screening ships to join in the assault against Japan.

It was the seaborne half of the total air campaign against the islands, the other half coming from hundreds of Superfortress bombers from the Marianas, aided by other hundreds of medium and light bombers based on the islands and land masses of the Pacific. They were to join a single great bombing and interdiction offensive that would break the Japanese and leave the country as defenceless as possible against the invasion.

The targets were airfields, any and all that were known or could be spotted. Warships and merchant shipping were to be attacked. Military installations and naval bases completed the roster. The area covered was to extend throughout the island empire, from Kyushu in the south, Hokkaido in the north.

The offensive opened for the Navy on 10 July, with a strike on the airfields in the plains around Tokyo. By now, the Americans had such a degree of air superiority that the fighters, although they still flew as escorts on strikes, carried bombs and were part of the strike force.

After the first Tokyo raid, the Navy shifted its attention to the northern regions of Honshu and Hokkaido, hitting airfields and shipping. They went back to Tokyo on 17 July, then pounded Japanese shipping at Yokosuka, the big naval base. They struck ships on the Inland Sea near Kure on the 24th, and attacked airfields on the northern end of Kyushu Island the same day. Then they moved up the Inland Sea to bomb Osaka and Nagoya the next day, and repeated the move northward on 25, 28 and 30 July.

The typical Hellcat bombing mission started with a climb to a cruise altitude around 20,000 feet/6100 m. (Individual aircraft varied, but maximum performance of the F6F series was obtained at altitudes between 18,000 ft/5500 m and 21,000 ft/6400 m, at that height, the Hellcat would cruise at a true airspeed of 205 to 210 knots with the engine in automatic lean mixture and turning about 2,000 rpm. (In these days of fuel shortages, it is interesting to remember that the Hellcat could cruise that way for an hour on just 75 gals/280 l of aviation grade gasoline.)

The mission had been launched before dawn, so that the planes would approach the coast while it was still dark, in order to catch the defenders by surprise. Running with the navigation lights on, the Hellcat formation would mark the 50-mile (80 km) distance from the coast and check the guns. Their flight plan would put them just over the coast at daybreak and, upon crossing the coast, the pilots flipped off their running lights and began the search for the familiar landmarks that would lead them to the target.

In the Tokyo area it was always Mount Fuji, with its characteristic shape and prominence, that gave them their bearings. At about ten miles from the target, the Hellcats would slide into a loose echelon formation, generally led from the left aircraft, and would cut back the power to start a long, quiet and speedy glide to the target. Somewhere around 10,000 feet (3000 m) the formation pushed over for the dive-bombing run. The pilots, if they remembered to do so, unlocked the landing gear and let it extend partially in a trail position, to serve as a stabilizing dive brake. The flight opened its formation to leave about 1,000 feet (300 m) between successive F6Fs in the dive. The pilots eyed their targets and the altimeter alternately, and when the gauge read about 3,000 feet (900 m), they pressed the bomb release on the control stick handgrip. A split second later they hauled back on the stick in a gut-wrenching pullout, jinking up and away if there were any anti-aircraft fire.

They did this, time after time, across the breadth and along the length of Japan. After the July 30 strike at the northern end of the Inland Sea, they stood down and moved south to avoid the typhoon that was roaring up into the area.

By the time they had returned, the top level commanders had been told about the highly secret operation that was scheduled soon. Hiroshima, they knew, was one city that was on the target list for a special operation, and the area

VF-3/USS YORKTOWN (CV 6) February 1945

VF-21/USS BELLEAU WOOD (CVL 24) September 1944

VF-6/USS HANCOK (CV 19) April 1945

VF-23/USS LANGLEY (CVL 27) March 1945

VBF-12/USS RANDOLPH (CV 15) May 1945

VF-27/USS INDEPENDENCE (CVL 22) March 1945

VF-17/USS HORNET (CV 8) March 1945

VF-29/USS CABOT (CVL 28) March 1945

VF-20/USS ENTERPRISE (CV 6) October 1944

VF-34/USS MONTEREY (CVL 26) July 1945

around it was to be kept clear for the Army Air Forces bombers. So McCain steamed well north of the doomed city. A few days after the news of that first nuclear weapon attack had electrified the world, TF38 again struck the Honshu and Hokkaido areas. Apparently, thought the Navy, the Japanese needed more convincing that they ought to surrender.

And they did, on 15 August, after a second city – Nagasaki – had vanished in a fireball brighter than the sun. At 0635 on the morning of the 15th, Halsey passed the word to his fleet. But he was too late to catch the first strike of the day which had been launched, according to custom, well before dawn and was at that moment dropping its bombs on the assigned targets. The second attack wave was on its way to the coast when it heard the commands radioed in the clear to all planes of the strike force: Return to base. Return to base. Do not attack; repeat, do not attack. The war is over; the war is over.

The Hellcats of VBF-87, from the *Ticonderoga*, were diving on Chosi airfield when the orders came through. All 12 planes continued, committed to the dive and the drop, ignoring the order. It would be easy to explain later, and besides, nobody really cared whether or not a few more bombs were dropped on the Japanese.

All through the target areas, the blue planes swung their noses around and headed back to their carriers. Several formations were jumped by Japanese fighters, who either had not heard the word, or who chose to ignore it in favour of one last opportunity to strike a blow for their country.

A mixed gaggle of VF-88 Hellcats from the *Yorktown* and Corsairs from the *Wasp* and *Shangri-La* were out on a fighter sweep with assigned targets in the Choshi Point area. The dozen Hellcats, led by Lt. Howard Harrison, had left their carrier in three flights of four. It was the first combat tour for many of the pilots; VF-88 had entered combat on V-E Day and had not yet accumulated that much experience in the real world of aerial combat. They had lost their skipper on their first day of combat, and had other losses since. It was felt to be a hard-luck outfit.

The twelve, with the lead flight high and the two trailing flights stepped down, penetrated a thunderstorm area. In its turbulence and low visibility, the formation was sundered. When they came out the other side, "Howdy" Harrison was leading a smaller formation, and they headed for a rendezvous point.

On the way, their radios picked up the return to base order and they began the easy turn back. Choshi Point had a lighthouse, and they decided to go down and shoot out the light as a last gesture, and then cruise past Fuji, to see that mountain without having to watch for Japanese interceptors.

They peeled off, blasted the lighthouse, reformed and headed for Fuji. In the distance they spotted a group of Hellcats headed toward them on a course that would take them back to the carriers. The Hellcats turned out to be a batch of Japanese fighters and they got one free pass at Harrison's formation. And then the sky was full of turning, diving, zooming planes, blue and metal, starred and red-balled.

That last dogfight, an unnecessary one, cost the Navy four pilots, including Harrison and the squadron "low-man," a pilot who was trying to log a fifth combat mission so that he would be eligible for a decoration.

The Hellcat was in combat with the U.S. Navy for a little less than two years. When the claims were added at the end of the war, the Navy said that the F6F had accounted for a total of 5,155 Japanese aircraft. The greatest number of those fell to the guns of the Navy's carrier-based Hellcats. Land-based Hellcats did considerably less damage to Japanese aircraft; they had other work to do.

Against those 5,155 victories was balanced the loss of only 270 Hellcats in combat during the war. The kill ratio is a little better than 19 to one, a phenomenal figure.

Its record as an escort for the strike forces was exceptional; the Navy lost only 42 dive-bombers and torpedo bombers to enemy air action during the Hellcat's day with the fleet.

The Hellcat seized and held air superiority over the Pacific. It defended the fleet and the strike forces with outstanding success. It achieved an enormous kill ratio over its opponents.

And, said Grumman's Dick Hutton, that's what we wanted it to do.